DISASTERSHOCK

How Schools Can Cope with the Emotional Stress of a Major Disaster

A Manual for Principals and Teachers

Disastershock Educator Collaboration Team

Disastershock:
How Schools Can Cope with the Emotional Stress of a Major Disaster
A Manual for Principals and Teachers

This book contains ideas, suggestions and procedures relating to health care. They are not intended as a substitute for consulting with your physician or mental health provider. The authors are not engaged in rendering professional advice or services to the individual reader of this book. The authors shall not be liable or responsible for any loss or damage allegedly arising from any information or suggestion in this book. While the authors have made every effort to provide accurate internet addresses and other contact information at the time of publication, the authors do not assume any responsibility for errors or changes that occur after publication. The authors do not have any control or assume any responsibility for third-party content. The authors do not license the creation of derivative works from this book or its translation into any other language without the express written consent of the authors.

Cover Photo Credits
    Forest fire photo by Jean Beaufort
    Hands in circle: Adobe stock picture
    Children with Globe by Getty Images
    Covid-19 photo by Tedward Quinn
    Hurricane photo by FEMA Photo Library
    Flood Photo by Chris Gallagher

ISBN 978-1-952741-28-9 ebook
ISBN 978-1-952741-31-9 paperback
© Institute for School-Based Family Counseling
2021

TABLE OF CONTENTS

INTRODUCTION: THE CRITICAL ROLE OF SCHOOLS IN COPING WITH DISASTER

Research indicates that "when adequately prepared, schools can and do buffer the negative impact of disaster" (Tobin, 2019, para. 1). This book is intended to help school communities cope with Disastershock; "the emotional stress that adults and children experience following a disaster" (Gerrard et al, 2020). It is our hope that this resource will provide you with hands-on, meaningful ideas that can equip you and your school to cope with disaster related challenges.

Children are particularly vulnerable to trauma caused by natural and person-caused disasters, but school personnel who model ways of effectively coping with stress can have a calming effect on students that facilitates their ability to learn following a disaster. School personnel are widely viewed as community leaders by the parents, guardians and families of school students. There is evidence-based support for the positive effects that school personnel can have on children and youth during disasters. In Appendix 1 you will find some of the important studies demonstrating how principals, teachers, and other school personnel play a valuable role in helping students to cope with disasters and trauma.

School environments are unique contexts that have the ability to facilitate the healthy development of the whole child by planning for ways to address their social, emotional, physical, and cognitive domains. In an effort to help children who have experienced trauma in their lives, many schools are adopting practices that build trauma sensitive school environments and approaches to teaching and learning so that students feel safe and can engage in the learning process. For example, teacher-student relationship building has become a high priority for many schools. Relationships that young people have in school have the potential to serve as protective factors that can ease the symptoms of trauma related to a disaster. We encourage you to take a moment and consider your current practices and initiatives that address the social-emotional needs of your learners. Your work in this area will serve as a foundation that you can lean into and build upon as you address a crisis. During a disaster, a school community needs additional coping strategies for school personnel, coping strategies for students, and coping strategies for the school-family community. The sections that follow seek to provide you with these coping strategies.

Part one, *Coping Strategies for School Personnel,* identifies the signs of stress that may be impacting administrators, teachers, and school support personnel. The section offers ten hands-on suggestions for ways to provide support for these critical school workers so that they can have the knowledge and emotional resources to then provide needed support for students and their families.

Part two, Coping Strategies for Students, is designed to equip teachers with needed knowledge and skill to help students cope during a disaster. When it comes to student academic growth and well-being, it is the teacher who has the most influence on this growth. Therefore, the role of the teacher and the support they provide during a disaster is absolutely invaluable.

The first two sections of part two will help teachers identify how stress may be impacting a student's ability to function in the classroom and provides advice for how to help students understand and cope with their stress. The last two sections are designed to help teachers to be more thoughtful about how to craft a classroom environment that will help students to learn during a stressful time and how to embrace pedagogical innovations that will help reduce student stress.

Part three, Coping Strategies for the School-Family Community begins with how principals and teachers can help reassure parents and caregivers. Embracing families and community partners in support of student well-being begins by equipping principals and teachers with messages that they can share with families to help them develop and maintain a helpful perspective as they walk together with their children through a disaster. The COVID-19 global pandemic, has highlighted the critical role of families/caregivers in the educative process of students. Such partnerships are vitally important to helping students weather a crisis and return to thriving personally, as well as academically.

Capitalizing on ideas that meet the needs of your school setting: As you read through this *Disastershock* publication, we encourage you to make note of action steps that you can take on behalf of your school. Identify who you might contact in your district to help provide you with support. Your action holds great promise to make a difference on behalf of children and adolescents. For additional resources, we invite you to visit the Disastershock website at https://www.disastershock.com/

PART 1 COPING STRATEGIES FOR SCHOOL PERSONNEL

HOW TO IDENTIFY WHEN SCHOOL PERSONNEL ARE STRESSED

Teaching is a stressful profession requiring multi- tasking, commitment, care and support for the students in their classroom and colleagues in the school. Following a disaster, schools and their personnel are an important anchor and safe haven in the affected community for children and adults. This can be a significant stressor and responsibility for school personnel.

The infrastructure of a school is the principal and school clerical staff. Following a disaster, they are the point personnel for multiple emails, texts and phone calls that are usually very challenging in content. Families look to schools for support and resources which presents an enormous challenge for the personnel. The principal assumes more of a role as "jack of all trades" and is expected to know the answers to not only school resuming but to individual student's needs. They are the forefront of a school and it is very difficult both physically and emotionally to meet their own needs as well as the school staff and the community needs.

Teachers have worry and concern not only for the academic achievements of their students but also for the welfare of their students and their families. They may have frustration in contacting and connecting with their students when virtual learning is possible. Digital availability and literacy of the students is a significant concern and stressor. School personnel may also experience secondary trauma as they provide support for those affected by trauma. School personnel have their own personal and family trauma in a disaster but the secondary trauma adds to the litany of stressors and the burden that they carry. Following a disaster, teachers try to connect with their students whether in a brick and mortar school or on a virtual platform.

The workload and need to multitask increases. Teachers are required to continue academic learning at a time that emotional and mental health concerns are heightened for not only the school personnel but for the students and their families. Teachers also need to adapt the curriculum to the modality of teaching that they will be using. Virtual teaching requires significant alterations of not only the material to be taught but also a platform for teachers to receive the student's work.

As school personnel return to whatever format of a classroom is possible, often their personal stressors are heightened. First to consider is whether the personnel have their own basic needs of shelter, food and clothing. The health and safety of their family members following the disaster is a significant component that affects their ability to be present and teach. The work-life balance may be strained as teachers adapt to significant changes in their working environment as well as their own and their families' needs.

Following are signs of stressed school personnel:

Overwhelmed physically and emotionally

Decreased attention and focus across multiple settings and environments

Decreased motivation

Signs of depression and anxiety

Absenteeism

Irritability and mood swings

Increased fatigue that affects daily functioning

Lack of organization with curriculum

Decreased productivity

Disorganization in daily schedule

Decreased availability to students and families

Disengaged from students

School personnel, including teaching and administration staff, are processing their own traumatic stress in a disaster. It is a challenge to be a "front-line worker" in a disaster environment. One is pulled between their own family obligations, their students' and families education needs, and their own safety and physical and emotional needs. Best practice is to have ongoing administrative support and guidance for self- care and wellness for all school personnel. This is best if it integrated throughout a school year at all times rather than focused on a response to a disaster. Wellness is a theme that needs to resound on a continuous basis for a healthy school environment for all personnel as well as students.

WHY IS TEACHER SELF-CARE IMPORTANT?

In all likelihood, teachers of children impacted by trauma and especially natural disasters may also have been affected by the traumatic events, either directly or indirectly. Therefore, caring for others who have experienced the trauma may not only be a stressful experience, but may compound the teacher's own reactions. In addition to helping children manage their emotions, it is equally important for teachers to care for their own emotions. It can be extremely helpful for teachers to talk to others about their own experiences, and get support where necessary.

Caring for young people who have experienced traumatic events can also have an impact on the carer (in this case, teachers). The impact on the teacher or person caring for the young person can involve feeling physically and emotionally worn out, feeling overwhelmed by the young person's trauma and reactions and experiencing traumatic stress of their own. This is also often referred to as 'compassion fatigue' or 'secondary traumatic stress'. Such reactions are not a sign of weakness. Rather, they are the cost of caring for and helping others.

There is some overlap between the reactions demonstrated by young people following trauma and those of teachers who are experiencing 'secondary traumatic stress' or 'compassion fatigue'.

Signs that may indicate teacher distress/secondary traumatic stress:
- Decreased concentration and attention
- Increased irritability or agitation with students
- Problems planning classroom activities, lessons and maintaining routines
- Feeling numb or detached
- Intense feelings, intrusive thoughts or dreams about a student's trauma (that don't reduce over time)
- Symptoms that don't improve after a couple of weeks

It is equally important to ensure that teachers look after their own welfare, as well as their students' welfare. It has been demonstrated that teachers who look after themselves and manage their own stress levels are more equipped and able to manage student behaviours and difficulties. Teachers who are stressed or experiencing strong emotional reactions will find it harder to react in calm and constructive ways to students who are demonstrating difficult behaviours. Below are some tips for teacher self-care.

Monitor your own reactions, emotions and needs.

Be aware of any signs of PTSD or distress that you might be showing.

Seek out support for yourself (in the school and/or community).

If your signs persist for longer than two or three weeks, it might be a good idea to seek further assessment or assistance from a health professional. Find your support system. Just like students, teachers need to protect themselves from becoming isolated. Your support system can be used to support your own emotional needs, or also to support you in supporting the young person (of course while maintaining confidentiality of your students). Talk to other teachers, ask for support from your administrators, work in teams, and establish or maintain your external support systems.

Seek help for your own trauma-related distress. Just like students, teachers may also need to seek further assistance to help manage emotions and reactions following traumatic events. Teachers who were also involved in the trauma or teachers who have other unresolved traumatic experiences are at greater risk of developing 'compassion fatigue'.

Use positive coping strategies to manage emotions and distress.

Try out calm breathing techniques, muscle relaxation, imagery (relaxation)

Challenge unhelpful thoughts that cause you distress. Try and generate more helpful thoughts and positive coping statements.

Look for resources to help you try new coping strategies. There are many good books, CDs and websites which can teach you calm breathing, relaxation techniques and how to challenge your unhelpful thoughts.

Maintain a structured classroom environment.

This is a good thing for children and teachers. Be prepared for daily classroom activities (and make sure the children are aware of these). Schedule relaxation or quiet times each day.

Plan ahead where possible, and have back up strategies for difficult situations. E.g., If you plan to spend some time talking to your students about the traumatic event, it may help to plan for the school counsellor, guidance officer to be present, to arrange time away from classes, or to have resources available to offer children or parents.

Maintain a healthy lifestyle.

In addition to the general benefits of a healthy lifestyle, teachers who have healthy eating, exercising, relaxing and sleeping habits are more likely to be able to manage their own stress and emotions as well as their students' behaviours. Being physically healthy allows teachers to remain calmer, and respond better to student stress and difficult behaviours.

Make time for yourself, family and friends.

Part of a healthy lifestyle includes maintaining your mental health. A big part of this is making time for yourself, family and friends. Everyone (teachers included) needs time out for themselves, to relax, have fun and enjoy themselves. Allowing yourself this time keeps you mentally fit and makes it much easier to manage your own stress and to help students manage their stress. Sometimes it is necessary to actively schedule these times in, rather than just waiting for others to do this. Try and organise fun activities every week, and spend a little time each day doing something for yourself. This might even be as simple as taking 30 minutes to read a book, taking time out to have a relaxing bath or spending time playing games with your family.

Spend time with students who have not experienced traumatic stress.

Sometimes it can help to spend time with students who have not experienced traumatic stress and to involve yourself in other aspects of your students' school lives.

Where can teachers find more information and help?

When teachers are concerned with their own emotional well-being, or feel as though they might benefit from further assistance, there are numerous ways in which you can seek help. Look for mental health support resources. There may be support provided through your school organisation, through state or country government employment, or as part of your employment. Teachers may choose to visit a mental health professional available in their area.

There are now also many excellent online self-help resources that can be useful for adults who would like some help in managing their emotions, maintaining a healthy lifestyle or generally adjusting following traumatic or difficult situations. Look up internet based resources in your city or country. A good place to start is the International Society for Traumatic Stress Studies which will give you access to many online resources (ISTSS.org).

TEN METHODS FOR SCHOOL PERSONNEL TO COPE WITH DISASTERSHOCK

If you are suffering from any of the symptoms of Disastershock described earlier, you may wish to try several of the ten stress reduction methods listed in this section. This is very important because if you as school personnel are distressed, you can hardly expect your students to be relaxed. When students are in the presence of principals, teachers, and school staff who are able to remain calm, this has a calming effect on students. We recommend that you select two or three methods that appeal to you most, and practice them several times a day. Most can be done in under 5 minutes and are known to be effective through extensive research. For most of these methods to work, you must practice them each time you start to feel stressed. They can be done before you come to school and also before you meet with students or other staff. Some can be done unobtrusively during a class or school meeting.

Method 1: Deep Breathing

This is the procedure of reducing tension in your body through practicing slow, deep breathing. This is a method you can use any time you feel tense or anxious. It is best practiced sitting or lying where you will not be disturbed. If you feel uncomfortable at any time, stop the exercise.

Let's try it.

Take a slow, deep breath through your nose for two seconds: 1 - 2.

Now hold your breath for two seconds: I - 2 and let it out slowly through your nose for two seconds: 1 - 2.

Now repeat, breathe in for two seconds: I - 2, hold for two seconds: I - 2, breathe out for two seconds: I - 2.

Now go to three seconds: Breathe in: I - 2 -3. Hold: I - 2 - 3. Breathe out: I - 2 - 3. Now repeat: breathe in: 1 - 2 - 3. Hold: I - 2 - 3. Breathe out 1 - 2 - 3. Now continue deep breathing with a 3 second interval until it feels comfortable.
When you feel ready go to 4 seconds. Breathe in 1-2-3-4. Hold 1-2-3-4. Breathe out 1-2-3-4. Now repeat: Breathe in: 1 2-3-4. Hold 1-2-3-4. Breathe out: 1-2-3-4. That's excellent.

When you feel ready, try 5 seconds.

You should now be breathing slowly and deeply. If you wish, you may extend your breathing intervals to 6, 7, 8, 9 or 10 seconds. Remember to stop if you feel uncomfortable at <u>any</u> time. Practice this deep breathing for at least 5 minutes. You can use this method whenever you feel tense - when you are alone, while your class is busy with an activity, or during a meeting when others are talking. Because of the brevity and the ease with which this exercise can be taught, this may be a useful one to teach students and staff to use before a class or staff meeting begins.

Method 2: Brief Muscle Relaxation

This stress-reduction approach works by having you tense then relax each of your major muscle groups one at a time: hands, arms, face, chest, legs. It is also called progressive muscle relaxation because of the systematic way relaxation will spread throughout your body. If you feel pain at any time while doing this exercise, stop and try a different Method in this book.

A first way to try this is to concentrate initially on tensing and relaxing your hands and arms. Let's try it:

Take your right arm and hold out your hand like you were a traffic cop stopping traffic. Your arm should be stretched out with your palm facing away from you and your fingers pointing up towards the ceiling. Bend your fingers back towards you until you feel tension in your arm. Hold the tension for 5 seconds 1..2..3..4..5. Now let your hand and arm relax. Slowly lower your arm until it rests easily at your side. Repeat this one more time.

Next repeat this using your left arm and hold the tension for 5 seconds 1..2..3..4..5. then relax your hand and arm. Repeat this one more time.

Now return to your right arm and make a tight fist and bring your fist up close to your right shoulder. Tighten your right arm by pressing your fist close to your shoulder while keeping your fist tight. Hold the tension for 5 seconds 1..2..3..4..5. Now let your right arm and hand slowly relax and move to a resting position at your side. Now repeat this one more time.

Next, repeat this using your left arm and fist and hold the tension for 5 seconds 1..2..3..4..5 then relax your hand and arm. Now do this a second time.

This hand and arm only muscle relaxation only takes about 5 minutes to do. Nevertheless you should be able to feel the deep sense of relaxation it can produce in your muscles. If you find this is working for you there are many videos on the internet showing how you can extend Brief Muscle Relaxation to other parts of your body.

Another version of Brief Muscle Relaxation involves tensing and then relaxing several muscle groups in your body all at once for 10 seconds then suddenly relaxing them. Here is how you can try that while sitting by yourself:

Let's try it. Are you sitting comfortably? OK, here goes:

Make a fist with each of your hands and squeeze your fingers together tight... tight... tight.... Place your fists against the outside of your thighs and push in so that you are squeezing your knees together. Push, push, push.

Squeeze your eyes shut tight and squeeze your lips together. Suck in your stomach and hold it, tight... tight....

Now press your knees and legs together as hard as you can. Hold all your muscles tight for 5 more seconds 1,2,3,4,5.

Now relax. Let all your muscles go completely limp. Let yourself be like a rag doll. Notice the contrast in how your muscles feel. Notice the sense of warmth and calmness spreading through your body.

Now try it again. Make a fist with each of your hands and squeeze your fingers together tight... tight... tight...

Place your fists against the outside of your thighs and push in so that you are squeezing your knees together. Push, push, push. Squeeze your eyes shut tight and squeeze your lips together.
Suck in your stomach and hold it, tight-tight....
Now press your legs together as hard as you can. Hold all your muscles tight for 5 more seconds: 1,2,3,4.

Now relax. Let all your muscles go completely limp. As you do so take a slow deep breath, hold it and let it out slowly. Think the word CALM to yourself. Let yourself be like a rag doll. Continue to breathe slowly and deeply as you notice the sense of warmth and calmness spreading through your body.

You may find it helpful combining this method with Method 1: Deep Breathing. You can use this method-to relax when you are alone (but not when you are driving).

Method 3: Monitoring Stressors and Your Stress Level

This method involves accurately identifying the things that are causing you stress (we call these "stressors") and keeping track of the degree to which you are experiencing stress. If you don't know that you are feeling stressed, then you won't know when to practice your stress reduction methods. If you don't know exactly what is stressing you, you won't know where to direct your stress-reduction methods.

Let's start with stressors. Some common stressors caused by disasters are:

- Daily reports on the numbers of persons who are sick or died.

- Not feeing safe to leave your home.

- Pictures of damaged buildings.

- Hospital and ambulance pictures of the sick and injured.

- Reading about how people died.

- Seeing homes on fire or being destroyed.

- Thinking where you live is not safe.

- Not knowing where other family members are.

These are only a few stressors that might be affecting you. A stressor may be something you see or something you just think about. Whatever it is, it triggers your stress. If you find yourself feeling tense or anxious, try to identify the stressor triggering your stress reaction.
Did you just watch the news and see a picture of damaged property? Are you thinking about the victims? Once you know the source of your stress you can bring into action specific stress-reduction methods to lower your stress.

Next, identify how stressed you are. If you are not aware of any feelings, look at your behavior. Are forgetting things, acting irritable, having trouble sleeping, can't sit still?

These are signs of stress. Try to develop an awareness of your feelings: are you feeling numb, depressed, sad, afraid, helpless, angry, or guilty. Label your feelings. See if you can connect your feelings with a specific stressor (for example, an image of an injured or sick person). It helps you to understand your feelings when you identify the stressors that trigger your feelings.

Rate your tension level using a I to 10 scale. Make 10 the most tense you have ever felt, and 1 the most relaxed you have ever felt. What is your tension rating right now?

Keep track of your stress levels by rating your tension level several times during the day. Notice the times when your tension level goes up, and use some of the other stress reduction methods to bring it down.

Method 4: Thought-Stopping

Thought-Stopping is a method for shutting off unpleasant thoughts and images. You can use this approach when you keep having an unpleasant thought or image over and over. The thought or image may be very serious (such as thinking about someone who died) or it may be less serious but nevertheless very upsetting (for example a colleague speaking to you in an abrupt or irritated manner). If you can't seem to turn the thought or image off, then you might find this method helpful.

Let's try it.

The moment you find yourself thinking of your unpleasant thought or image, pinch yourself lightly on the arm and think the word STOP!

Take a deep breath and, as you slowly let it out, think the word CALM and imagine yourself in the most peaceful scene you can think of (for example, lying on the beach, resting at the mountains or the lake, or relaxing in your backyard).
For at least 20 seconds imagine your peaceful scene in as much detail as you can. Concentrate on imagining the scene of beauty about you.

Let your body develop a sense of relaxation as you breathe slowly and deeply. (See Method 1: Deep Breathing.)

For this method to work, you must use it *every time*, repeat: *every time* you start to experience the unwanted thought or image. The method works by interrupting the unpleasant thoughts or images and by replacing them with positive images.

Method 5: Relabeling

Relabeling is the method of using positive words or labels to describe something you have been labeling in a negative way. Instead of saying: "The glass is half-empty" you say "The glass is half full." You look for the Positives in a situation and emphasize them. This will help to reduce your stress. For example, if you see a picture of a damaged building, instead of using negative labels such as:

"This is awful."

"So many died there."

"This is horrible."

Search for positive labels:

"There were so many courageous volunteers."

"Not that many died compared to what was first expected."

"Think of the many lives that were saved."

"The heroic rescues of many persons."

Similarly, when thinking about the disaster overall, use positive labels:

"Comparatively speaking there were fewer deaths than was feared."

"Most buildings were not damaged"

"We can learn from this disaster to _____."

Ask yourself this question: *"This disaster is clearly a terrible situation, but how can I grow as a person facing this enormous difficulty?"* Some possible answers you might come up with are:

"I can help others who are worse off than myself."

"Although it will be difficult, I can work on developing courage in facing adversity."

"I can remember who I am and what my core values are."

Whenever you find yourself using a negative label, search for a positive one.

Method 6: Positive Self-Talk

This is the method of thinking *Positive Coping Statements* to yourself before, during, and after your encounter with a stressor.

Here's how it works. Let's suppose you know you are going to see something that really stresses you - for example, you have to drive to work and you get very stressed whenever you pass over a bridge that you imagine will collapse. This is a common fear for anyone who has experienced an earthquake.

To use Positive Self-Talk, make a list of some positive things you can think to yourself **before** you drive over the bridge, **while** you are actually on the bridge, and **after** you have passed over the bridge.

For example, as you approach the bridge you could think:

"There is the bridge, but I can handle it."

"Everything is going to be alright."

"I can manage my stress by breathing slowly and deeply."

"I've handled this successfully before."

While you are on the bridge you could think:

"I can handle it."

"I'll be over in a few seconds."
"Relax and breathe deeply."

"I can stay calm."

"Everything will be alright."

After you have passed over the bridge, you can think:

"Congratulations!"

"I did an excellent job."

"I managed my stress."

"I did my breathing well"

You will find it helpful if you prepare these Positive Coping Statements and then concentrate on thinking them in advance. Concentrate as you go through the 3 stages of encountering a stressor: before, during, after. This method works by interrupting the flow of negative images and thoughts that you might be having as you encounter your stressor. You can use Positive Self-Talk with any stressor you have to encounter directly (for example, passing a spot where someone died or having to enter a grocery store where there are other people during a pandemic).

Method 7: Positive Imagery

Positive imagery refers to imagining doing something that is very pleasant. This interrupts negative images and thoughts that stress you. If you are feeling generally stressed, you may wish to *Fantasize Having a Mini-vacation.* (Don't try this if you are driving.)
Let's try it. Imagine you are on holiday in your favorite vacation spot. If you are at the beach, feel the warmth of the sun on your skin, sense the warmth of the sand beneath your beach towel, feel the breeze gently blowing across your body, listen to the waves gently splashing. Try to experience being there through all your senses. Continue this for about 5 minutes.

If you have to pass by a stressor directly (such as passing a place where someone was injured or died), try imagining yourself doing something pleasant that involves movement. Imagine yourself jogging; visualize yourself dribbling a basketball and shooting for the basket; imagine skiing on a field of snow and notice the snow spraying up over the tips of your skis as you make your turns.

This method works by focusing your imagination on re-experiencing in detail some pleasant activity.

Method 8: Challenging Irrational Beliefs

This is the method of writing down beliefs about the disaster that you think are irrational (but which you still believe) and then challenging these irrational beliefs by finding rational beliefs that contradict them.

Some common irrational beliefs you might have are:

"My family member will get sick and die"

"The highway bridge is going to drop on me."

"Another disaster will occur tomorrow."
"My students are too stressed to learn from me."

"My house is going to collapse."

"I'm going to be killed."

"I am surrounded by nothing but horror."

These are all examples of irrational beliefs because they tend to catastrophize and overemphasize a negative point of view, and ignore positive information.

Give it a try.

Identify any belief you might have about the disaster that you think is irrational or excessively negative.

Write it down on a piece of paper under the heading: Irrational Beliefs.

To the right write the heading Rational Beliefs.

Under Rational Beliefs try to write out some more positive, rational beliefs about the situation.

For example,

Instead of: *"My family member will get sick and die."*

Write: *"If my family member does get sick, they might recover and be fine."*

Instead of: *"The bridge is going to collapse."*

Write: *"The chances of any bridge collapsing under me (or anyone) are very remote, there was only 1 bridge that collapsed in the disaster."*

Instead of: *"My students are too stressed to learn from me."*

Write: *"Although my students are experiencing a lot of stress right now, my teaching will give them something else to focus on that is positive and this will help them."*

Write: *"The chances of any bridge collapsing under me (or anyone) are very remote, there was only 1 bridge that collapsed in the disaster."*

Instead of: *"A huge flood (fire, earthquake, etc.) will occur tomorrow."*

Write: *"A huge flood (fire, earthquake, etc.) may just as likely not occur tomorrow. The last time a disaster like this occurred was 20 years ago."*

Instead of: "I am surrounded by horrors."

Write: *"It is true that many have died and much property has been damaged; it is also true that I am alive and there is much of life to appreciate; this is a very special community and I can be proud of how its citizens are courageous and loving in helping each other."*

The heart of this method lies not in glossing over negatives, but in seeing the truth: that in reality there are positives even in the most tragic of circumstances.

Method 9: Restoring Positives/Reducing Negatives

When we are caught up in dealing with a crisis, it is easy to forget to continue doing those pleasurable activities that naturally reduce our stress. For us these include: eating take-out, going for a walk, lying in a lawn chair in the sun in the backyard, watching a favorite TV show; playing with our dogs and cats, listening to music, watching football and baseball, and enjoying the company of family and good friends (even if on zoom or the phone if we cannot be physically present with them), to name a few.

You may find it helpful to identify relaxing activities you used to do before the disaster and then encourage yourself to start doing them once again. By re-engaging in these pleasant activities you will be interrupting the flow of negative images and thoughts caused by the earthquake and you will be reminding yourself that disaster is only a very small part of life.

In addition to restoring positives to your life, you may find it helpful to reduce the negatives. If you feel stressed by pictures of disaster damage, don't look at them right now. Turn off the portion of the news that shows disaster coverage. Don't look at unpleasant pictures on the internet. For the time being listen to some music rather than the news. Don't take in more negative images and information than you can handle. If there are unpleasant people in your life that you can avoid right now, avoid them. Identify negative persons and things that depress you and reduce your contact with them for the time being.

Method 10: Developing a Sense of Mastery Through Action

An important source of stress caused by a disaster is the feeling of helplessness it produces in most of us. A disaster strikes without warning and we have no control. There are, however, some things you can do to reduce stress caused by feelings of helplessness. These are activities that you do to develop a sense of mastery or control over yourself and your environment with respect to dealing with disasters.

First, you can develop a *Disaster Preparedness Kit* for yourself and your family. These contain materials such as water, food, a battery-operated radio, flashlight, first-aid kit, blankets, and a written plan describing how family members - if separated - will get in touch. You might want to keep one of these kits in your house and also in your car. In dealing with a pandemic like the 2020 Covid-19 pandemic, having hand sanitizer, disinfectant, and surgical masks that can be used to protect family members, and a plan to maintain social distancing when in a grocery store, is critical. Being prepared in this fashion will reduce your sense of helplessness. You will know that if another disaster occurs, you have basic survival materials to protect your family and yourself.

Second, you can volunteer to help those affected by the disaster. You could give a homeless family temporary quarters if you have a spare room. You could give blood to the Red Cross. You could donate food, clothing, or money to a community agency helping survivors. Any of these volunteer activities will give you a sense of mastery over the disaster by giving you the sense that you are reducing its negative effects on others. On a more personal front, you can check in with friends and extended family members (using mail, email, phone, or video conferencing) to let them know you are there to support them.

Third, you can become an expert on disasters and disaster survival by reading all you can on your particular disaster. For example, for persons coping with earthquakes, one book we like is called *Peace of Mind in Earthquake Country* (Yanev & Thompson, 2009. Knowing about earthquakes if you live in an earthquake prone area can reduce your sense of helplessness. For example, during an earthquake should you stay inside a building or try and get out in the open? Where is the safest place to stay during a tornado? Finding the answers to questions like these will help you build a sense of mastery.

Finally, we recommend you become an expert in stress reduction as this will give you a sense of mastery over your feelings and tensions. There are many fine books on stress reduction as well as videos on youtube that demonstrate stress reduction approaches in detail. You can find some of these on our website disastershock.com.

We recommend that you try several of the above ten stress reduction methods, and try them more than once. These are not the only stress-reduction methods you should consider. There are likely some calming approaches that have worked for you in the past. For many persons these might be: prayer, listening to certain types of music, talking to a close friend or family members, exercising, playing a sport, etc. We recommend you also use what has worked for you in the past. There is no "one size fits all" approach to stress reduction. If you find that these methods do not reduce your stress and that you are experiencing very high levels of stress, we strongly recommend that you seek counseling from a qualified mental health professional.

PART 2: COPING STRATEGIES FOR STUDENTS

HOW TO IDENTIFY WHEN STUDENTS ARE STRESSED

What is stress? It is a reaction of mind and body to particular unsettling experiences. Many stress feelings and reactions are shared in common by people of all ages. Children's stress responses in the event of a disaster may be obvious or subtle. Most importantly, children's distress may be expressed differently depending on the developmental age of the child. Special attention is required to identify and meet the needs of students.

The most common reaction by students of all ages to a disaster is fear and anxiety. A child is fearful of a reoccurrence of the disaster. Another common fear is that the child or a family member might suffer injury in a reoccurrence. Connection to family is the child's safety net. The child should be aware of where immediate and extended family members are. Encourage families to consider using internet video (e.g. FaceTime or Zoom) to connect with family that is out of the area. Another step to alleviate a child's anxiety is remind families to rehearse what the family members might do in the event that there is another disaster. What are some safety precautions the family will take at home? The families might have a safety drill at home similar to a school's fire drill. Encourage families to identify a plan if the disaster occurs when the child is at school. Who will pick up the student? These precautions might help students of all ages feel more secure and safe.

During a disaster, parents are stressed too. The parents' fears and anxieties are passed on to the children. An adult has more experience in coping with such stress, and has more sophisticated coping mechanisms to draw on, whereas children often do not. Therefore, it is important for a teacher to remind parents to recognize the emotional needs of the child. A child may be scared and frightened. This anxiety often does not disappear by itself. Teachers can acknowledge that the fear and anxiety expressed by the young person are very real. You need to understand what the specific fears are if possible. The only way to find this out is to talk to your students. Social-Emotional curriculums might be very helpful with strategies to help the students express their trauma. This might help and support the behavioral and emotional presentation of the child in the classroom.

Listen to what your student's specific fears are. Talk to your students about their feelings. Find out what your students think has happened. Your students may have been inundated with television, social media and internet reports which may have blown the crisis out of proportion. You need to state the facts of the disaster. Continue to listen to your students they will express either directly or indirectly fears associated with the disaster. The most important responses to a child that you can make are to listen, to encourage the student to communicate and to continually reassure the child by speaking directly to him/her.

It is important to understand the issues that families face following a disaster that directly impact a student's ability to focus and attend to learning. The first concern is if the student's family has shelter, food, clothing and other very basic needs. Negative behaviors are often a result of trauma that is experienced in a disaster and may have been a concern before. This is a signal that something is wrong that is impacting the student.

Many students may experience a loss of interest and motivation in school. This reaction may range from fear of separation, to the anxiety that the school is not safe, to a lethargic response to school activities and peer interaction. It is even more challenging when school is only on-line and communication with teachers is by video only or not at all. Often students will go on line for school but refuse to have the camera on them. Another common response seen in children of all ages is regressive behavior. A student might revert to prior behaviors exhibited at an earlier developmental stage because it might seem more safe. The present situation is unsettling so the escape to a previous secure state is reassuring. This is where the "class clown" may re-enter the classroom. Other behaviors seen in students of all ages may include difficulty expressing their worries, often confused, feeling annoyed much of the time. These responses are common and such behaviors may persist for a long period of time following the disaster. Mental health challenges are very common in students' responses to disasters.

Children of different age groups have specific stress reactions to a disaster. A child who is 5 experiences different vulnerabilities than does a child of 14. For the purpose of this book, the age groups will be divided into Preschool (ages 1-5); Early Childhood (ages 5 -11); Preadolescent (ages 11 - 14); and Adolescent (ages 14 -18). Table I summarizes the most common stress responses for the different age groups.

Children in the Preschool age group (ages 1 - 5) are particularly vulnerable to the disruption of their safe and secure environment. Their development has not reached a level of conceptualization that permits them to understand a disaster. Preschoolers lack the verbal skills to communicate their fears and anxieties. As a result, a Preschooler's stress is best identified by exhibited behaviors. These behaviors may be indirect so special attention to the child's needs is important. Typical regressive responses which are considered normal are thumbsucking and bedwetting. A 5 year old may have stopped sucking his thumb at age 3 and spontaneously begin this behavior again. This is normal but should not continue indefinitely. Another response is a fear of the dark and nightmares. This is particularly heightened immediately following the disaster. It is also tied in with the Preschooler's fear of being alone and this fear increases at nighttime. The Preschooler might exhibit a behavioral response such as an increase in clinging to the parents.

Table 1. COMMON STRESS RESPONSES OF CHILDREN TO DISASTER

_____

_____

Common Stress Responses of Children (all age groups)
Fear of recurrence of the disaster
Fear of injury
Fear of separation
Fear of being alone
Sleep disturbances
Night terrors
Loss of interest in school
Loss of interest in peers
Regressive behavior
Physical symptoms (headaches, stomach aches)
Isolation
Sadness

Stress Responses of Preschool Children (ages 1-5)
Thumbsucking
Bedwetting
Fear of the dark
Night terrors
Increased clinging
Expressive language difficulties
Loss of appetite

Loss of bladder and bowel control

Stress responses of Early Childhood (age 5-11)
Whining
Clinging
Separation anxiety
Fear of the dark
Nightmares
Avoidance of school
Poor concentration
Increased aggressiveness
Withdrawal from peers

Stress Responses of the Preadolescent (ages 11-14)
Appetite difficulties
Headaches
Stomach aches
Psychosomatic complaints
Sleep difficulties
Nightmares
Loss of interest in school
Loss of interest in peer group
Increased rebellion at home
Aggressive behavior

Stress responses of Adolescents (age 14-18)
Headaches
Stomach aches
Psychosomatic complaints
Appetite disturbance
Sleep disturbance
Decrease in energy level
"Irresponsible" behavior
Increased dependence on parent
Withdrawal from peer group
School problems

In the stress responses of the Preschooler (ages 1-5), a disaster increases the child's separation anxiety. Another stress symptom is speech difficulties. Language is a relatively new developmental milestone and may suffer in ways such as stuttering, stammering and difficulty in expressing in a fully coherent manner. A Preschooler's loss of appetite is another stress signal. Loss of bladder or bowel control, particularly in the older Preschooler, will often indicate stress. The overriding anxiety among Preschoolers is fear of abandonment and fear of being alone.

Stress responses in middle childhood (ages 5 - 11) are more generally indicated by regressive behavior. Behaviors such as excessive whining and clinging to the parent are common. This group may have an increase in separation anxiety from the parent which is more typical behavior of a preschool child. The child may refuse to walk into school and cling to the parent or refuse to participate in on-line classes. The 5 to 11 year old may begin to experience a fear of the dark and nightmares. The nightmares may be connected to past events of the disaster as well as fear of future occurrences. Many such stress behaviors are exhibited at school. A child may want to avoid school and even if encouraged to attend school may lose interest and have relatively poor concentration in school. The parent needs to let the teacher know what symptoms of stress have increased that may impact the attention and focus needed for learning. This also applies to on-line school during the disaster. Other behavioral signs range from an increased aggressiveness to a withdrawal from friends and family. In order to determine these stress signals, the parent and teacher should try to recall what the child's normal behavior patterns were prior to the disaster. In this way the deviation from the norm can be assessed because each child's so-called "normal" behavior is different. What might be observed as a stress signal for one child is not necessarily true for the next child.

The stress reactions in the Preadolescent (ages 11 - 14) include behavioral differences as well as physical responses. Physical symptoms that signal stress are complaints of headaches, stomach aches, vague aches and pains and psychosomatic complaints. The preadolescent may have difficulty sleeping and wake up with nightmares. Another physical symptom might be loss of appetite. In a preadolescent child, the physical symptoms may be coupled with school problems. The child may complain of a headache in the morning and stay away from school. This could also be symptomatic of loss of interest in school and withdrawal from peers, which is also a normal stress reaction. Other children will express stress signals in a more aggressive way. These behaviors include increased rebellion at home and refusal to participate in family or school activities.

Reactions to peers are particularly significant with the preadolescent and range from withdrawal to aggressive behavior with friends. It is important to help the preadolescent by affirming that the physical and behavior responses are normal and shared by other people, particularly his or her peers.

The Adolescent (ages 14 - 18) stress responses also include physical and behavioral signals but this age group's stress is increased because they are caught in the middle (between being viewed as children who need to be attended to and as adults who can cope on their own). The Adolescent is not an adult but an older child who has developmental needs, as do the other age groups. Some adolescent young people feel guilt and shame when they are unable to take on adult roles during or in the aftermath of a disaster. These feelings increase the adolescent's feeling of isolation.

Physical responses include headaches, stomach aches, and possible psychosomatic complaints, such as rashes. Appetite and sleep disturbances are also common. Another symptom might be a decrease in energy level where the once energetic and enthusiastic adolescent becomes apathetic and disinterested in previously satisfying activities. Suicidal ideation is a concern at this age. Listen for any mention of a suicidal plan.

Let students know that you support them and are always willing to listen. As a teacher, communicate that you are open and available to listen to them and any concerns that they have about themselves or others. Students then will be more apt to share concerns that they have learned about peers through social media particularly self-harm media posts. Behavioral stress responses often show up in the adolescent's interaction with peers because peers are central to this developmental stage. If the school is temporarily or even permanently closed due to disaster damage, this can have a profound stress effect that must be identified and directly addressed. Other behavioral stress responses might be irresponsible behavior - a "nothing can affect me" attitude, or dependent behavior at the other end of the spectrum where the adolescent becomes less independent and tends to cling more to the family. It is most important to listen and talk to the adolescent and encourage the student to reconnect with his or her peer group.

The most important way to determine the child's stress reactions in any age group is to listen to the student's fears and anxieties. Although these fears may seem childish or insignificant to an adult they are very real to the child. If your student is one who is shy about communicating then you may have to initiate the discussion.

A disaster is not a situation where we can say it's permanently over. We must live with the possibility of another disaster, as well as continue to live with the ramifications of the original disaster, whether it is the closing of a school, rebuilding of a home or deaths in the family. The effects don't disappear immediately.

It is important to note that the majority of children will cope and overcome the fears and anxieties of a disaster. But some children continue to suffer the trauma. If the physical or behavioral stress symptoms do not diminish after a few weeks or months depending on the disaster or if the symptoms become worse, it is time to seek professional help. A mental health professional can assist your students in coping with stress and trauma reactions. Utilize the resources at your school – the school mental health professional and other support personnel.

TEACHING STRATEGIES FOR REDUCING STUDENT STRESS

When children and adolescents face a disaster, such as COVID pandemic, they feel vulnerable and experience anxiety and concerns related to danger and safety. They fear for their integrity and that of their loved ones. Students may experience a broad range of reactions following a disaster, including behavioral changes, emotional distress, attention difficulties, sleep disturbances, physical symptoms, anxiety and fears. These reactions can cause distress that can interfere with adaptive coping, and impact on school performance, classroom behavior, and social and emotional development of children.

Educators play a key role in helping their students to manage stress, to regain calm, and to feel safe and supported: socially, emotionally, and academically. Teachers are in an excellent position to help children after disasters as they are significant adults in children's lives; they are familiar with developmental processes; and, they are likely to notice emotional and behavioral changes, academic difficulties, and functional impairment in their students. They are critical in recognizing the signs of traumatic stress, promoting resilience and helping students to manage reactions to stress.

How can teachers help their students to manage traumatic stress? Create a sensitive trauma-learning environment by: promoting a safe and welcoming climate; seeking to create a structured and predictable learning environment that minimizes unnecessary trauma and loss reminders; focusing on building positive relationships; and, applying evidence-based techniques and practices that promote resiliency, stress management and adaptive coping.

School-based interventions that teach students skills in cognitive reappraisal, mindfulness meditation, relaxation response, and positive psychology have been shown to improve stress coping among students. Attending these evidence-based interventions, a pool of strategies and techniques has been selected to help you support students suffering a "disastershock".

1. Identify students' symptoms of stress

The first step in applying stress management strategies is to assess stress levels of your students' group. Some students may be more vulnerable than others to a disaster and need further intervention during crisis. The following strategies can help you identify students' stress symptoms:

Learn about the symptoms and signs of stress in children and adolescents who are going through a disaster. In the previous section (Part II – Section 1), you have a detailed description of these symptoms according to your students' age. You can create a check-list of stress symptoms, and use it to guide your observation of your students' behavior in the classroom.

Use your students' prior knowledge to identify changes in their behavior, emotional reactions, and school performance associated with stress trauma.

Identify those students who may be most vulnerable to the disaster. Consider the life history of your students to identify risk factors (episodes of depression, anxiety, learning difficulties), histories of previous trauma (abuse, domestic violence) and current situations that may be an obstacle for the child face disaster (isolation, less supervision because of caregivers' work schedules).

Monitor and follow up on the symptoms and signs of students' stress, to verify their magnitude and duration over time. Seek help from a health professional – counselors, school nurse, school social worker– if you notice that these symptoms are severe, persistent, and are interfering with children's daily activities.

Consider doing an activity with your students that allows them to express their feelings regarding the disaster. This practice should be done in an environment of trust and support for children. In the case of young children, you can ask them to draw a picture about what happened. For older schoolchildren, you can ask them to make a collage or write a news story about what happened. In the case of adolescents, you can propose holding a reflection circle in which each student can express their feelings and concerns about the disaster.

2. Creating a sensitive trauma learning environment

Creating a learning environment that recognizes disaster's emotional consequences involves reinforcing a series of actions and strategies that promote support, a sense of safe,

connection, and predictability for students. Consequently, it is important to:

Create a welcoming experience for students. Students should feel welcomed and valued. Do this by praising students for participation, as well as by allowing relationships and well-being to take priority. Begin the class with a check in activity. Share with your students a poem or a short lecture with a positive message, or practice a five minutes' meditation. Encourage your students to reflect about how they feel by writing in private their feelings and concerns. Also, you can lead a discussion about what's happening with the crisis, and how the situation is being handled. Students will feel safe and supported if they perceive that their teachers care about their well-being.

Establish a school routine. Exposure to a disaster creates feelings of unpredictability and uncertainty. That is why it is important to create a school routine that allows students to regain a sense of stability and foresight. Assist your students in the use of the school agenda and calendar, so that they organize and plan their daily and weekly activities. Create rituals to start and end the class. For example, share with your students one grateful moment, give a positive message or practice a mindful activity before or after checking assignments.

Maintain clear and fluid communication. In times of disaster, it is important to expand communication channels with students and their families. Students should feel that they can communicate with their teachers with ease. Also, it is important to provide information as clearly as possible, and in student-manageable amounts. Use visual schematics, images, and reminders to make it easier for your students to get information.

Be flexible. Adapt the tasks and assessments. During crisis and disaster, students can feel assignments are more overwhelming. Present instructions in smaller bites when necessary, and encourage students to ask clarifying questions. Use diverse forms of assessment that allow you to monitor the progress of the students and to evaluate the learning process. Address academic and behavioral issues with empathy and support.

Use positive feedback. Highlight and value the effort of students to carry out their tasks and progress. Use a moment in class for students to assess what they have learned and shared. Help them to highlight the positive, and provide opportunities to improve those areas where they had difficulty.

Promote dialogue. Provide a space for your students to share what they understand and do not understand about disaster. Be curious about their experiences. Take advantage of these moments to clarify any misinformation, and use the technique of reframing negative thoughts.

Create and communicate the school's emergency response plan. It is important that the school has a plan for managing a disaster (earthquake, flood, epidemiological situation worsening in a pandemic). After a disaster, students may not want to go to school for fear of a new disaster, and they fear being separated from their family. That is why teachers have to communicate to students and their families that the school has a plan to handle the disaster. Specify how students' physical and psychological health will be maintained, how the school is going to connect with family, and how any future problems will be handled.

3. Promote connectedness and hope

In the face of a disaster, contact with others may be restricted by distance, natural catastrophes, and diseases. Restricted contact with loved ones and other people is one of the greatest stressors for human beings. That´s why it is important to:

Let your students know that they can discuss their concerns and fears with you. Encourage them to connect and seek help from educators, counselors or other trusted adults.

Provide moments when students can enjoy the company of their peers. Introduce play times and pleasant activities between partners. Consider putting students together in small groups to work on projects or activities.

Encourage your students to connect with their friends and loved ones. If the contact with others is restricted, help them find ways to connect remotely, by phone or video chat.

Share stories of hope. Share with your students how communities have handled past disasters. Share stories of people who have managed to overcome the current crisis. Focus on messages of hope, and how others have helped them to face it. Help your students identify and share with others practices, activities or rituals that give them hope.

4. Use socio-emotional learning practices and wellbeing activities.

Socio-emotional learning practices and wellbeing exercises can be incorporated into your classes and you will give your students the opportunity to feel valued, practice self-compassion, and affirm their sense of competence.

Recognizing emotions and feelings. Encourage your students to recognize their emotions, and how they connect to the body. Indicate that there are no good or bad emotions, but that an emotion is a way of reacting to situations. That it is important to recognize them in order to be able to control them later. You can use a journal in which children can record their emotions and feelings. Model and normalize a range of emotions. Promote and value self-expression through different channels. Encourage them to express themselves by art, such as drawing a picture about how their day is going or role playing the most important thing that happened to them that day.

Empower your students. Help your students to discover their active role in facing disaster. Help your students identify daily actions they do through which they care for or offer help to their family and friends. Teach them that a hug, a smile, listening to another, a call or a message, can all be actions that help others to feel better and, consequently, help them face the crisis.

Strengthen resilience. Help students to identify their strengths. How much have they done today? How have they faced the difficulties? Teach them to treasure their achievements.

Strengthen self-compassion. Help your students understand that they may feel stressed, distracted and tired, and they may consequently experience greater difficulty doing things they used to do easily, or that they make more mistakes than usual. Help them understand that our bodies, emotions, and brains are busy dealing with disaster. Therefore, we may make mistakes more often or be less motivated. Teach them to forgive themselves and appreciate that they are, in fact, fighting this difficult situation. So, don`t forget to be flexible and adapt tasks and assessments.

Express feelings of gratitude. Teach your students to identify the many things they are grateful for in their lives: a hug, parents' love, the caress of their pet, or a sunny day. Help them express feelings of gratitude to others. You can take a few minutes in your class to ask your students to draw or write in their journal one thing they are grateful for each day. You can make a gratitude circle in your class, and ask your students to write a phrase of gratitude towards their classmates. Get in the circle, and, then, encourage students to share their thoughts.

A treasure box. Help students to create a box in which they can treasure those objects, memories, phrases or thoughts that make them feel happy, and calm. They can turn to that box whenever they feel sad or hopeless.

5. Promote healthy habits.

Help your students identify and practice healthy habits. Talk to them about the importance of a healthy diet, sleep hygiene, exercise and contact with nature. A healthy and balanced diet that includes vegetables, fruits and dried fruits plays a central role in maintaining our physical health and a good level of energy. Sleeping between 8 and 10 hours a day and practicing good sleep routine- such as meditating for a few minutes before going to bed, reading a book and avoiding the use of electronic devices one hour before going to sleep - improves the quality of sleep. Share videos, lectures, games that allow your students to understand how a healthy diet and a good sleep are keys to coping with the crisis, as they help us to be physically and mentally healthy, improve performance in daily activities and help manage stress.

Talk to your students about the importance of doing regular physical exercise. It has been documented that 30 minutes per day improves blood circulation in the brain and increases the secretion of neurotransmitters that help create neurons which improve learning and memory. Also, doing physical exercise improves mood, increases energy level, improves attentional performance, and helps control stress levels. In facing a disaster, it is important to allocate two or three hours of weekly school planning to do regular practice of sports, gymnastics, or dance. Furthermore, teachers can model a mini physical breaks in class, such as a three minutes' stretch.

Include in your school activities a walk in the park, an outdoor activity, introducing the practice of mindfulness in contact with nature. It has been documented that 20 minutes of contact with nature decreases of cortisol (stress marker) in the blood and improves the immune system. Promote activities where students can use their five senses to be in contact with nature.

Take time out of your class to help your students establish a healthy daily routine, in which they can balance their schedules for study, rest, exercise, eating, and sleep. Provide students with resources, such as a daily check list and agenda, to help them establish a routine that suits family resources and activities. Talk to their parents or caregivers about the importance of maintaining a routine, so that children and adolescents are physically and psychologically healthy. Suggest that the family stick to a daily routine as much as possible. Also, suggest activities that parents can share with their children: go for a walk in the park, watch a movie, share a board game or go biking. Communicate that in times of crisis, we must prioritize connecting with our loved ones.

6. Use mindfulness and relaxing techniques.

Many schools have adopted mindfulness in their classrooms. Using these effective methods following disasters can help your students to relax and cope with tension, anxiety or fear.

Deep breathing

Focusing our attention on the breath helps us feel calm and relaxed. The deep breathing technique that you learned for yourself (Part I – Section 3) can be taught to your students. But remember that when you teach breathing or any calming exercise, it is essential that you are calm and relaxed. The technique is simple and consists of modeling to your students how to breathe slow and deep. In the classroom or on the playground, ask students to sit comfortably. Then, breathe slowly in through your nose for 3 seconds, hold your breath for 3 seconds, and, then, breathe out slowly for 3 seconds. Repeat this several times so your students get the idea. Then, ask your students to breathe with you. You can ask them to count each breath silently or to place their hand on their abdomen to feel the breath on their body. This helps students focus their attention during the exercise. Repeat this exercise with your students for a minute or two. Then reflect with your students on the experience. Talk about how they felt, what they felt in their mind and body, and how breathing has helped them. Take this time to let them know that they can use this exercise whenever they feel stressed, anxious or worried. Focusing attention on breathing is a way to regain tranquility when fears or anxiety flood us. Deep breathing helps us to quiet our mind and our emotions, allowing us to improve our performance in any activity (studying, playing an instrument). End the exercise by asking them to draw a picture of the experience or to write a word or phrase that helps them feel calm.

Once the students know this technique, you can use it to start or end a class, in transitions or at times when you perceive that your students are restless, anxious or stressed.

You can adapt this technique according to the age of your students. For example, with young children, you can teach them to breathe deeply by playing with soap bubbles or blowing up balloons. With older children, you can combine breathing with movements; for example, instruct them to raise their arms when they breathe in, hold them up while holding their breath, and when they breathe out to drop their arms. You can imitate animal movements or superheroes. With teens, you can combine deep breathing with sports or martial arts movements.

Muscle Relaxation

This technique consists of contracting and relaxing the muscles of the body. It is very useful for relaxation. You can teach this technique to your students through the game of "the statue and the rag doll". Teach your students how to tense the muscles of their body, imitating a stone statue, and then to relax them, imitating a rag doll. Practice this technique sitting down. Show your students how to contract all the muscles in your body and to keep them contracted for 5 seconds just like a statue. Then relax your muscles like a rag doll. Repeat this exercise three or four times and then talk to them about how they felt. What happened when they turned into a rag doll? Did they feel calm or stressed? Ask them to draw the rag doll and write the word calm. Show them that they can use this technique when they feel stressed or nervous. They can practice this exercise at home, or when they are alone.

Looking carefully

This technique helps students to fix their attention on a visual point and learn to control their distractions. This technique can be done in the classroom or outdoors. Tell your students that on many occasions, we look without paying attention and we stop seeing important things. Especially when our mind is restless, or when we are anxious or stressed, we stop observing our surroundings. Focusing our vision on an object can teach us to improve our attention and control distractions. Ask your students to do the following exercise: ask your students to fixate their eyes on an object for a minute. If they get distracted during this exercise, they have to make an effort to fix their eyes on the object again. You can use any object you have in the classroom, but it should not be moving. Finally, discuss the experience and ask if it was difficult for them to focus on the object. What was distracting them? Teach them that attention can be trained like any muscle, and that it must be exercised consistently. Once the students have mastered the technique, you can introduce a new exercise: observe their surroundings calmly and quietly for a minute. Then, ask them to try to discover objects, details, colors that they had not observed before. An excellent idea is to practice this exercise outdoors. Instruct your students to practice this exercise at home or in the park, that the goal is to observe in silence and calm, trying to discover objects or details not previously perceived.

You can vary this exercise by training auditory attention. Do the exercise by asking your students to close their eyes, and to listen to the sounds around them. You can ask them to focus on a particular sound and then ask them to discover new sounds.

Use your imagination to create a place of calm and well-being

This technique consists of imagining a place in which we have felt calm and relaxed. Ask your students to close their eyes for a few moments and to imagine that place. It could be any place in which they have felt relaxed and calm, which could be the beach, a park, their garden, or their room. Instruct them to use deep breathing while imagining that place.

Also, guide their imagination by telling them to focus their attention on some sound or object in the image. Talk to them about how they felt, and what they felt in their body and mind. Let them know that this technique can be used when they feel tense or stressed.

Identify and stop negative thoughts

This technique consists of recognizing and stopping negative thoughts. Help your students identify their negative thoughts, and recognize how they are manifested in their body, emotions, and actions. You can ask them to keep a record of these thoughts in their journal. Then, you can teach them some techniques to stop negative thoughts. One technique is to tell your students to imagine that their thoughts are in a river and that when the negative thought appears, transform it into a leaf or piece of wood and let it flow into the river. As the thought drifts away, instruct it to use deep breathing. Also, you can use some of the relaxation techniques you have learned such as muscle relaxation, looking carefully, or attentive listening. Also, you can use your imagination to return to your place of calm for a minute and to combine it with deep breathing.

Reframe your negative thoughts

Reframing negative thoughts helps your students see something positive in a situation that they consider negative. You can teach your students to rephrase their thoughts in a more positive way. You can start by taking some negative thoughts of your own and showing them how to reformulate them. For example, "people who get sick from coronavirus die." You can rephrase it by saying, "if people use social distancing, wear masks and sanitize their hands, it is very likely that they will not contract the disease. Most people who get sick get better. In addition, we have vaccines that will help us not to contract the virus". Encourage your students to identify a negative thought and share it. Help them rephrase it. The objective of the technique is to show the students that their thinking is partially true, but that they have misunderstood positive aspects of the situation. This technique helps students reduce their tension and strengthen their sense of hope. Do not neglect the negative thoughts of your students, but motivate them to express them, so you can help them reformulate them in a more positive way.

In our web site www.disastershock.com you will find other useful resources – lectures, videos, expressive art activities – to help your students to handle a "disastershock".

It is important to point out that suggestions and techniques mentioned in this section do not have to be all done at the same time. Rather, use your understanding and reflection to select a pool of techniques that best suits your students at a particular time.

Finally, don't forget to take every opportunity to highlight progress of your students in the management of stress techniques and adaptive coping. In a crisis or disaster situation, you should help them treasure their good deeds and achievements. It is necessary to reinforce their value and their active role in the face of disaster. Likewise, when your students show a good understanding of these techniques, you can encourage them to lead these simple activities for the class. This increases buy in and also creates community.

Classroom Expectations and Management During a Disaster

Set clear and firm limits/expectations of behavior

During times of recovery, it is important for children to return to normal routines and functioning. As part of this, it is important that teachers do not change expectations relating to schoolwork and behavior, and rather that you make adjustments where necessary to the way you deliver classroom activities. For example, if children are having some difficulty maintaining concentration, it may be necessary to change to 15 or 30 minute blocks and incorporate physical activity in between (e.g., stand up and shake it out) to stimulate attention and concentration.

Acting out and misbehaving is one behavior that children and adolescents may demonstrate in response to natural disasters and traumatic events. It is important for teachers to set clear expectations of behaviors and to communicate these to the young person. Generally, young people respond well to clear boundaries and routines which involve firm and clear limits for behavior and clearly stated (and implemented) consequences for misbehavior. The emphasis should be on consistent and logical consequences, rather than punitive consequences.

Acting out and misbehaving are a common reaction to trauma, but also generally a common behavior in young people. Therefore, it is always important to explore the origins of the problem behavior before jumping to conclusions about diagnosis or implementing consequences or discipline strategies. The fact that the young person might be acting out (even a year after the trauma) does not mean that the young person is demonstrating a behavioral disorder (e.g., attention-deficit disorder, conduct disorder). Even the most disruptive behaviors can be expressions of trauma-related anxiety.

It is important to implement consequences when expectations of behaviors are not met. However, the emphasis should be on logical consequences, rather than unrelated consequences. For example, a child who hasn't completed a homework activity can be asked to remain with the teacher at lunch time to complete homework; A child who refused to share with another child is asked to give the toy to the other child and apologize for their behavior; A young person who has used bad language can be asked to spend lunch time searching for other words (in the dictionary) they could use to express their emotions.

Use a 'buddy' or 'support' system

Many schools have a 'buddy' system. Often teachers may implement a buddy system following trauma whereby students are paired with other students to ensure that each student has a support person while at school. Often this is implemented in the hope that children are not left alone, and to provide sources of emotional support to each child. The buddy system may be more appropriate for younger children, but teachers might want to think of ways in which teenagers can be encouraged to maintain their own social support systems.

Although the buddy system might be most useful immediately following the traumatic event, it may still be beneficial to consider for some children over time. Some children have ongoing difficulties, some may not like to be alone, some may require ongoing emotional support and others may simply enjoy team environments.

 A buddy or support system might be useful for various classroom activities (e.g., going to the bathroom, relaxation time, group activities). Over time, buddy systems can be turned into more 'support' or 'companionship/friendship' systems, whereby children are encouraged to use their buddy as sources of emotional or academic support.

Safe 'relaxation' spaces

All classrooms can benefit from having safe spaces that are specifically for young people to use when they are experiencing difficulties in the classroom. For some classes, this might be a specific room adjoining the classroom, whereas for others, this might be on seats outside the classroom. These areas can be used when children or adolescents need some time to calm themselves down, or if the teacher needs some time to talk to students individually. Placing some comforting children's books or quiet activities in this space will give children something else to focus on while they take some time out from the demands of the classroom.

It may be necessary to set up procedures for the young person to gain permission to leave the classroom, or visit the relaxation space. Adolescents may even request permission to visit the student welfare co-ordinator or school nurse. For younger children, this can be through nonverbal requests (e.g., placing a particular color card on the corner of their desk to indicate to the teacher that they would like some time out or 'relaxation' time).

Provide choices – regain control

Often, during the traumatic event, young people may feel a sense of powerlessness or loss of control. Traumatic events are usually beyond the control of the young person, as are the consequences that follow. One strategy that might be useful is to provide young people with choices or input into some classroom activities. Giving children choices and involving them in decision making can help restore their feeling of control.

Examples of ways in which children can be offered choices or be involved in decision making:

Providing suggestions regarding fun classroom activities

Choosing between various classroom activities (eg, books to read, science experiments to perform)

Choosing between assignment topics (for older children, choosing between different essay topics)

Helping to select and organize fund-raising activities.

Anticipate difficult times and plan ahead

It is likely that children and adolescents may re-experience some of their symptoms, or experience some distress at important milestones. Anniversaries of the event, birthdays of lost family members, holiday times (Easter, Christmas, Mother's Day, Father's Day) can all be especially difficult for young people.

During these times, it is possible that the young person might demonstrate an intensification of emotional difficulties and problem behaviors, or might even develop new behaviors or emotions that cause distress to the young person or class. Where possible, it may be a good idea to plan ahead and pre-empt these occasions and provide additional support where appropriate. For anniversaries, strategies may need to be discussed with other school teachers, administrators and even family members of the students. It is important to consider the wishes of the families affected by the trauma.

Teachers and schools may plan events to coincide with anniversaries, with an emphasis on survival stories and positive events since the trauma.

Teachers may also approach individual students where appropriate or necessary and use some of the skills discussed above to work out whether the young person will require extra support during this time.

Prepare children and adolescents for situations which may trigger reactions

Some young people, although generally functioning well, might still be affected by sudden and significant events or triggers. It can be useful for teachers to warn or prepare children for any sudden events. For example, students may need to be warned about upcoming fire drills or sirens that might be tested. Teachers may also need to let children know if they are about to do anything sudden, like turning off all the lights, or making loud noises.

For older children and adolescents, it may be useful for teachers to anticipate upcoming events which may trigger responses. For example, teachers may be able to prepare students in advance regarding upcoming assignments or activities that may trigger emotions or memories of the events (e.g., if an upcoming class includes discussion of natural disasters, science class which discusses concepts related to flooding, English class which involves investigation of news/disaster stories). In these instances, some young people might need to be given alternative activities they can participate in.

Focus on strengths and positives

For many families, there can be a long time following the trauma where the focus remains on the traumatic event, getting their lives back together and dealing with the problematic reactions that follow. As a result, it can be very easy to focus on the negative things going on in the young person's life, including problems managing emotions and behaviors. Often little attention is paid to the positive behaviors or coping strategies the young person is showing.

Providing positive reinforcement or praise for things the young person has done well not only makes the young person feel good about themselves, but also demonstrates to the young person what type of behaviors they should continue to engage in. Acknowledging and reinforcing strengths, positive behaviors and coping strategies can be a particularly important and easy strategy for teachers to practice and implement. This can be as simple as offering praise to students when you notice a positive behavior, or personal strength they have developed or demonstrated.

Help students to build a support system

One of the most distressing outcomes following traumatic events and natural disasters is the loss of community. It is important for children and teenagers to build a strong support system. Sometimes it is important to make sure they have multiple support sources at school as well as home.

Teachers can help young people to identify who they can talk to about difficult situations and any problems they are having. Some children may not be aware of who the student welfare co-ordinator, youth worker or school counsellor is. Teachers may also be able to help students identify other school staff they feel comfortable talking to, should their classroom teacher not be available. For example, they may feel comfortable talking to their sports teacher, the principal or school nurse.

HOW TEACHERS CAN USE THE EXPRESSIVE ARTS TO HELP STUDENTS COPE

Creativity can be a powerful tool used to help students address the emotional and psychological struggles they may experience when faced with difficult circumstances. Utilizing the expressive arts in the classroom can be supportive of not only students, but also you, their teachers, in times of crisis, during a transition, or in the aftermath of traumatic events. Expressive arts refers to visual art, music, drama, play, dance, movement, or poetry. This section will highlight how creativity can be used as a therapeutic coping mechanism in schools and detail a number of expressive arts directives that you can use to help support your students' resiliency, self-expression, and connection to themselves and others.

During times of prolonged stress, our nervous systems may become stuck in fight or flight, making things like critical thinking, taking in new information, memorization, decision-making, problem-solving, and focusing very difficult. Pair these struggles with the issues kids today are already facing and it is no wonder many are having a difficult time. Offering expressive arts modalities like painting, drawing, singing, movement, and even play can help calm their nervous systems and serve as powerful ways you can support their success, in and out of the classroom. Engaging in the arts allows for the fight or flight mechanism to be turned off and for students' right brains to be activated. This is essential because our right brains are responsible for things that can help make learning easier like imagination, creativity, emotion, intuition and nonverbal communication.

Our goal is to teach our children to be creative thinkers and problem solvers, equipped with as many tools in their toolkits as possible so that they are ready to face any challenges that come their way. By fostering creativity in the classroom through the use of the expressive arts, you are helping to facilitate increased self-esteem and curiosity, as well as re-instill a love of learning. Unlike with multiple choice tests, there are no right or wrong answers when it comes to artistic expression and the focus is always on the process, never the product. Allowing students to choose and experiment with various types of art media utilizes choice-based learning and helps foster a sense of personal autonomy and agency. For students who don't do well with standard ways of learning like tests and reports, an introduction to the arts can open up their world to new and different areas in which they can excel and express themselves without judgements or critiques. The change in focus from "thinking and judging" to "feeling and exploring" will be a welcome change for most.

As you introduce your students to the art directives detailed in the following pages, it is important that you stress they keep their focus on how they *feel* during each process, rather than on the outcome or how their art *looks.* You are offering them powerful means of nonverbal communication and it is important that their expressions be witnessed without assigning "value" to them based on appearance or skill level. For example, refrain from giving feedback that focuses on the aesthetic of the piece, such as, "That is beautiful!", or, "You're so talented!" Instead, focus on the energy behind the expression or how you feel when you witness it by saying things like, "I feel my body relaxing when I look at your art," "I find myself smiling when I look at the vibrant brush strokes used in your piece," or, "I love the authenticity and vulnerability behind what you have created!"

Lastly, you are there to facilitate the experience for your students and hold the space, not to show them how to do it. Again, with these art processes, there is no right or wrong, so this is a chance for you to take some pressure off of yourself as well, knowing that will be no grades or measures of learning. This is a time for your students to create and enact their own experience and gain mastery using their own natural ability to create. Every child is creative and your job is simply to create a nonjudgmental, open, compassionate environment in which they feel free and safe enough to explore. There are countless expressive arts activities that will work well either in a classroom or virtually, but you can start with these!

Creative Brain Dump

Who:
Students ages 8+
Teens

Why:
Emotions that are denied or suppressed can end up getting stored in the body and, ultimately, feel much bigger and cause more issues and distress. This directive is a fairly easy, straight-forward way to get pent up energy and emotions out of the body and onto paper or canvas. The result is that these uncomfortable feelings may feel less scary or overwhelming when seen in the form of art or words on a page.

What:
Have your students gather a piece of paper or a canvas (the larger the better, but work with what you have) along with an assortment of either colored markers, crayons, colored pencils or oil pastels. Please note that paint is not typically recommended for this, particularly watercolor, as the fluidity of the medium could provide too sensory an experience for someone already experiencing intense feelings and may end up "flooding" or overwhelming them with emotion. It is always important to notice how your students respond when using various art materials and to stick with those that seem to make them feel better, not worse.

Take a moment and invite your students to close their eyes and tune into how they are feeling in their bodies as they take three deep breaths. They can do this with their eyes open as well if that is more comfortable.

Things to ask your students to consider as they breathe:
- What sensations are you noticing?
- Where in your body do you feel those?
- Do those sensations have a temperature? Texture? Color? Name?

Next, invite your students to open their eyes and use their art materials to express the sensations that came up onto their paper or canvas. These expressions may include lines, mark-making, smearing, scribbles, or even words. Ask that they allow whatever comes up to come up without judgment or concern for how it *looks*. Instead, ask that they tune in to how the experience *feels*. Invite them to stand up or move their body in a way that feels right for them while they create.

The point is to allow all of the "stuff" that is flooding their brains and, consequently, affecting their bodies, to get dumped into their art.

Once the students are done with their visual expressions, invite them to dialogue with their art piece, either speaking aloud or writing down the exchange.

Questions for them to consider while dialoging:
- What does your piece have to tell you?
- What do you want to tell your piece?
- If your piece had a title or a name, what would it be?
- How do you feel in your body when you look at your piece?

Now that their difficult or overwhelming emotions are safely onto their canvases or papers, instruct them to create a "home, nest, or cave" for their pieces using whatever materials they have on hand (cardboard, tissue paper, construction paper, sticks, rocks, etcetera). Remind them that their art pieces need to fit inside their new home in some way, even if that means they fold or even crumple them up if that feels right.

Lastly, invite your students to place their" creative brain dumps" into their new homes and allow their pieces to take a little vacation for an hour, day, or a week (whatever they need) by placing them somewhere out of sight. This could be under or inside their desks or a cubby if you are doing in-person learning, or any place in their home that feels safe if you are doing virtual learning.

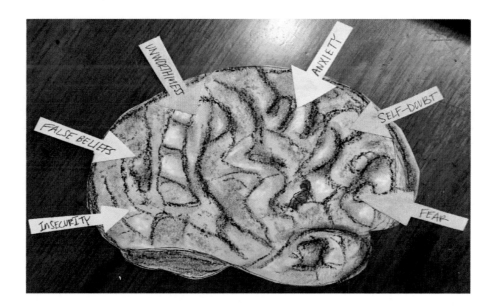

Instruct your students to take out their "brain dumps" the next time they are feeling overwhelmed by fear, anxiety, or panic and allow their pieces to serve as symbolic reminders that their troubling emotions are on a little vacation right now. Maybe even invite them to say to them out loud, "Thank you. I know you're trying to protect me but I don't need you right now. You're not helpful, so I've sent you off on a little vacation. I'll let you know when I need you again."

Invite your students to create a new "brain dump" whenever they feel that their emotions are running high and they need a place to put them. It is also important remind them that difficult emotions are allowed and *should* be felt and experienced, but then they need to be allowed to move on, rather than letting them get stuck.

Create a Superhero Self

Who:
Students ages 6-12
Students ages 12+
*When using with older students, you may replace the words, "Superhero Self" with "Alternate Persona"

Why:
This directive is designed to give students a sense of self-empowerment and agency as well as help regulate their emotions and connect them with a more helpful version of themselves.

What:
Ask your students to imagine a version of themselves that thinks and behaves in a way that would make them feel safer, less scared, calmer, or braver during stressful or traumatic situations. For fun, you can call this their, "Superhero Self!" For older students, ask them to consider an "Alternate Persona" or version of themselves that feels and behaves exactly how they would want to show up during a time of crisis—the healthiest or most helpful version of themselves.

Next, invite them to create a 2-D or 3-D art piece (painting, sculpture, drawing, puppet, etcetera) to represent this version of themselves using whatever materials they have on hand. Examples of materials could include construction paper, fabric, paints, markers, pipe cleaners, and clay, or simply pencil and paper. Give your students a good amount of time to focus on their creations, either in the classroom or in their own homes if you are doing virtual learning.

Questions you can ask your students to consider as they create:
> What characteristics does this version of yourself possess?
> For Example:
> - How do they move?
> - How do they talk?
> - What do they wear?
> - Do they have a different name?
> - What types of thoughts do they think?

Questions for older students could be:
> - What are the 3-5 main qualities this version of you would have?

- What habits would make up your day?
- What habits would you need to let go of?
- Would this version of you have a different name?
- What is keeping you from being this version of yourself on a daily basis?

Once your your students are done creating, ask them to make something three-dimensional that they can put on when in "superhero mode". Examples of this might include a mask, cape, crown, wand, face paint or headpiece. For older students, rather than create something to wear, you may ask that they dialogue with their Alternate Persona.

Questions for older students to consider as they dialogue:
- What does this other version of you want you to know?
- What message do you have for this version of you?
- What makes this version of you feel unsafe?
- Where does this alternative version reside?
- Is there a word you can say out loud that would summon this "other you"?

End by letting your students know they can access their Superhero Self at any time. Remind them that, the next time they are experiencing emotions that are troubling for them, they can call in their Superhero Self/Alternate Persona by putting on the wearable piece they created, adding to their original art piece, or even creating a" Superhero Sidekick". You should also stress that being a "superhero" does not mean denying emotions—particularly worry and fear—but rather, this persona is a reminder that they can also feel other things (courageous, calm, creative, funny, helpful, loving, etc.) The idea is to help them access more helpful emotions in a time of crisis, not to deny that a full range of emotions exist and are okay.

For older students, you can remind them that this version of themselves already exists and is in them and accessible at all times, regardless of outside circumstances. In difficult times, invite them to pretend like they are "playing a part" (fake it until they make it) until this new way of being, feeling, and thinking starts to become second nature and they truly embody the persona they created.

Anxiety Monster
Who:
Children ages 6-10
Teens

Why:
The objective here is to help students process their feelings and fears around the unknown. By personifying something that feels scary, making it more tangible and allowing them to dialogue with it can lessen the fear around it and give them a sense of agency over the situation.

What:
Ask your students to create an "anxiety monster" using any art materials they have on hand. Depending on what is available, this could be a drawing, sculpture, painting, puppet, or anything else they can imagine.

Questions to consider asking your students to help them create:
- If your anxiety were a monster, animal, or some kind of tangible "thing," what do you imagine it would look like?
- What color, size, shape, and texture would it be?
- Would it talk? What would its voice sound like?
- Can you give it a new name?

After your students have finished their creations, invite them to interact with their pieces by dialoguing back and forth.

Questions you may invite your students to consider while dialoging:
- What do you want to say to the anxiety monster? (or insert its new given name here)
- What does the anxiety monster have to say to you?
- Can your friends and family interact with it as well?
- Why do you think the anxiety monster is here?
- Can you tell the anxiety monster how life has been different for you since its arrival?

Next, invite your students to create a cave or "bunker" to house the anxiety monster so it can't harm them and suggest that they put it in its new dwelling and hide it somewhere out of sight. Again, use whatever materials you have on hand such as clay, construction paper, or a shoe box.

The next time fear or panic comes up around a situation that feels scary, remind your students that the anxiety monster is safely in its cave. Maybe invite them to dialogue with the monster more, if necessary. Allow them to release their emotions onto the monster. ("I feel overwhelmed by you!" "I know you're here to protect me but I don't need you and you have to leave!") Then invite your students to instruct the monster to go back into its cave. The idea is to give the students some sense of agency over this "invisible threat" by making it more tangible and something they can actually interact with and speak to.

Movement & Music Centering Exercise

Who:
Children ages 10+
Teens

Why:
During times of uncertainty and stress, one's body can become stuck in "fight or flight" and, in this highly aroused state, it is common to obsess over thoughts about the past or worry about the future. Bringing one's thoughts back to the here and now using sound, breath, body awareness, and movement can be very useful in calming the nervous system, regulating the body, and breaking up the cycle of rumination or catastrophizing.

What:
Ask that your students take some time to find music that they enjoy—perhaps a song or soundtrack that they particularly connect with. If you are doing in-person learning, then you will want to ask them the day before to prepare to have their music and some ear buds with them for the next class session. If you are doing virtual learning, you can either have them prepare their music ahead of time or allow them a few minutes to find some during your online class session.

Once the students have their music prepared and before asking them to play it, invite them to get comfortable where they are. If you are in the classroom, allow the students to find a spot in the room where they can have some personal space—either standing or seated to start. If they are in their homes, ask them to find a spot, either indoors or outdoors, where they can have some privacy and room to move.

- Next, invite your students to take a few minutes to close their eyes and connect to their breath. Instruct them to focus on the sensations in their bodies as their bellies and lungs fill up with air and they release the air slowly. Perhaps you can suggest that they try making a low "hum" sound as they release their breath and see how that changes their experience. Invite them to feel their body (or feet, depending on whether they are seated or standing) firmly planted on the ground and notice everything that is true about both themselves and their immediate environment in that moment. They can either state these awarenesses out loud, whisper them, or simply say them to themselves.

Examples of things you might encourage them to notice and "awareness statements" they might make:

"I notice that I feel calm and safe in this moment."
"I smell the wet paint from our art projects earlier today."
"I feel the warm breeze on my face."
"I feel my stomach move in and out as I take long, slow breaths."
"I feel my heart beating as I put my hand to my chest."
"I hear the sound of birds chirping."

Once you have given your students enough time to establish a sense of connection to their physical bodies and their surroundings, invite them to either put in their earbuds (if they are in the classroom) or mute their microphones (if they are learning remotely) and begin to play their music.

Ask that they first allow themselves time to sit or stand in stillness, focusing solely on the sounds they are hearing, inviting them to pay special attention to the rhythm, instruments, beat and lyrics of their music.

Next, invite them to turn their awareness to the difference in how they were feeling in their bodies in the silence before the music began and how they are feeling in their bodies now that their music is playing.

Examples of some of the somatic differences you might encourage them to note:

- Has your heart rate increased?

- Has your breath quickened? Slowed?
- Has your body temperature changed?
- Do you feel the urge to move?

After giving your students time to connect with the sound of the music and the physical sensations in their bodies, invite them to begin to move to the beat in whatever way feels good to them. Be sure to remind them to try not to focus on how what they're doing *looks*, rather, to keep their attention on how it *feels*.

Allow your students to get lost in the experience of moving their bodies in a totally free way (they may close their eyes if this helps) and engage in this exercise for as long as your class session allots for. Remind them that, if intrusive or worrying thoughts about the past or future attempt to come in, they can bring their attention back to the present moment as their bodies respond to the music. The idea is for them to practice grounding themselves and their experience in the present, as opposed to allowing their thoughts to wander to the distant past or an unknown future.

*Optional additional Step:

Invite your students to take out a large piece of paper and colored pencils, markers, finger paints, or whatever other art materials they have available, and to keep moving their bodies as they add color, lines, and marks to their paper. They may continue to keep their eyes closed as they do this, as to avoid get caught up in focusing on how the piece looks. Remind them to keep their attention on how the expression feels. The idea behind this final step is to allow them to transfer and express the energy they are feeling in their bodies from the movement and music exercise onto the paper. What will result in a visual expression of their energy in that moment. Allow your students to keep creating until you sense (or they report) feeling regulated in their minds in bodies and attuned to the present.

Immediate Environment Art Assemblage

Who:
Children ages 8+
Teens

Why:
Trauma can make our world feel small and cause us to get lost in our own anxious thoughts. Nature is one constant that we can turn to to help our mind focus on

something outside of ourselves, connect us to our immediate environment, expand our imagination, and help us feel grounded and centered.

What:
Creating three-dimensional art using objects found in one's immediate environment, particularly those found in nature, are referred to as *assemblage* or *nature assemblage.*
Invite your students to create their own assemblages by exploring their immediate environments and gathering any objects they find themselves drawn to. If you are in the classroom, this is a wonderful opportunity to get outside and, if you are doing remote learning, students can explore their own backyards. Challenge them to see their environments with new, curious eyes and to focus solely on their "foraging mission," putting all other thoughts or worries aside. The process of slowly gathering objects can serve as meditation when done mindfully and with intention so stress that your students take their time and not rush their exploration.

For students without yards or access to nature, you can invite them to become explorers in their own homes or bedrooms instead. Allow your students enough time to gather a variety of objects to work with (you may suggest that they use a paper bag, basket, or small box to collect their items in order to make foraging easier) and, when they are ready, ask them to find a flat area in which they can lay out their discoveries.

In addition to their found objects, you may also suggest that your students use collage materials as part of their assemblage. These can be words and/or images cut or torn out of magazines, newspapers, old books, calendars, or even junk mail. Next, invite your students to begin assembling their objects in a way that feels good to them, reminding them that this is an intuitive process with no "right or wrong." Do not have your student tape or glue anything down, allowing instead for this to be a fluid process and one that is impermanent.

Examples of things you might say to help guide them as they create:
- Imagine that your assemblages are little worlds you are creating where you get to decide how everything looks and feels.
- You have the freedom to change your world if you're not happy with it by moving things around, adding things, or removing things.
- Where might you place yourself in your "world" if you were to shrink yourself down and jump into your assemblage? What would you do? How might you feel?

Once students have had enough time to create at least one assemblage (some might work quickly and have enough materials for more), invite them to photograph their creations using their phone, a camera, or some other device. If you are in the classroom, perhaps you can photograph their work for them if phones are not allowed. Because their creations are not glued down and will be

disassembled, having a photo allows them to revisit their worlds whenever they choo

Lastly, invite your students to take apart their creations and either return their found objects back to nature or store their items in a box to be used in future assemblages. This process is meant to serve as a reminder that what is happening in the greater world is also impermanent and that difficult time will pass. This exercise's focus on nature and the use of items found in nature may also serve as an opportunity to talk about cycles of death and rebirth, if that feels appropriate.

Teachers, you are being asked to do extraordinary things under extremely difficult circumstances. In this section, the focus has been on how to help your students deal with prolonged stress using the expressive arts, but it is vitally important that you find ways to manage *your* stress as well. We invite you to consider using the arts in your own lives to process and express what has been coming up for you during these unstable times. All of the exercises detailed above can be utilized by adults as well and you may even do them along with your students. Modeling the importance of self-care and mental-wellness is, perhaps, the most important gift you can give them. Let the arts provide you with not only powerful, but fun, ways to enrich your lives and the lives of your students!

SCHOOL CHILDREN AS RESOURCES FOR OVERCOMING A DISASTER CRISIS

School teachers and children are health workers

The World Health Report 2006 published by the World Health Organization (WHO) defined health workers as "all people engaged in actions whose primary intent is to enhance health." This report reflected the health workforce crisis due to the devastation of HIV/AIDS, accelerating labor migration, and chronic underinvestment in human resources at the global level. The definition was created under such a critical situation and it writes that mothers are health workers for their children at home.

Under this definition, school teachers can also act as health workers, particularly during natural and human-made disasters. It is well addressed in this book as to how they can function as such roles. However, school children can sometimes act as health workers for themselves, their classmates, family members, and even their teachers.

After the Great East Japan Earthquake in Japan on 11 March 2011, school children took action to overcome the tragic circumstances even after losing their houses, friends, and family members. On 18 March, after a week of living in an emergency shelter at a school gymnasium, a seven-year-old girl (second grade in primary school) issued a unique wall newspaper. Her idea was, "I want to cheer up everybody in the shelter because people seem to be discouraged here." In the wall newspaper, she picked up only happy stories to share when she wrote. It was named "Fight," and her new friends in the shelter shared happy events. In the first issue, they wrote, "You (adults) are now living in unfavorable circumstances but let's fight for the future! We will also do our best." They reported many stories in the newspaper: "a volunteer team came from Osaka, and they made a warm and tasty pork miso-soup," "wonderful doughnuts were served to everybody for a snack," "we found pretty tulips blooming." In total, they issued 50 wall newspapers until 3 May, when most people moved to temporary housing. The girl who started the initiative says, "Because the people who read the newspaper talked to me with a smile, I was also encouraged."

We tend to believe school children are vulnerable, and it is school teachers who should help them. However, as shown in the above story, sometimes we can find an opposite direction during and after the disaster.

Child to Child Movement in the World

Such children's power and strength have been well known in Africa, Asia, and other resource-limited settings. In 1978, Dr. David Morley and Dr. Hugh Hawes conceptualized this as the child to child approach. As written on the website (www.childtochild.org.uk), "Child to Child is a pioneer of children's participation. Since the 1970s we've partnered with and trained the world's leading agencies to equip children with the skills to stay safe, stay healthy, achieve their potential – and have a voice in matters concerning them." It also mentions that "when children work together, they can change their world." In response to the COVID-19 pandemic, they have also created a special resource site (Highlighting Resources: ECD, COVID-19 Response - Child to Child).

To understand and strengthen the school children's potential must be one of school teachers' additional roles during a disaster. By doing so, it provides an opportunity for school children to help themselves and to help others. As many school teachers may experience during and after disasters, seeing school children's smiling faces is a priceless reward for their work. By being helped by school teachers, in turn, school children show their appreciation and their appreciation helps school teachers consciously or unconsciously. The value of being helped by school children should not be forgotten nor dismissed to make the school teachers' support longer-lasting.

Child to Child in Action

In addition to what teachers can do to school children during a disaster, school children can do a lot to help themselves and others. Often, children are better at finding the right ways to help one another. In particular, older children can help younger ones. They can craft toys, read stories, and teach songs and dances for the younger ones. Below are some more selected specific lessons learned from actions taken in Yemen (water and hygiene activities in Somali refugee camps), Croatia (to increase mine awareness), and other resource-limited settings.

Knowing

Children should:

- Know that the behavior of friends, family and other adults can be affected by stressful situations.
- Know that children need special affection and help to understand and express their feelings in disaster situations.
- Know that it is especially important to include children with disabilities in playing and other activities under challenging circumstances.

Doing

Children should:

- Participate in spreading health messages relevant to their situation.
- Organize and participate in sports, games, drama and singing activities to help themselves and others have fun.
- Identify and include children with disabilities in all activities.

Feeling

Children should:

- Feel concerned about the feelings of other children and adolescents who have lost family members or had other bad experiences.
- Feel able to listen to the worries of other children.
- Do not feel guilty when friends or family appear angry, depressed or withdrawn.

Dr. Frank Riessman's "Helper Therapy Principle" suggests, "when the individual provides assistance to another person, the helper may benefit." School children can become such an individual during and after disasters

HOW A TRAUMA INFORMED SCHOOL BENEFITS STUDENTS

In a 1997 landmark research study between Kaiser Permanente—San Diego, CA—and the Centers for Disease Control and Prevention—Atlanta, GA—with 17,500 middle class individuals, the concept of Adverse Childhood Experiences (ACES) was born. Originally focusing on obesity, weight loss and regain, co-researchers, Drs. Vincent Felitti of Kaiser and Robert Anda of the CDC, learned that many medical conditions were in fact connected to significant childhood traumatic experiences. Since then their work, the advent of ACES and the by product of toxic stress has reshaped the fields of medicine, mental health, public health and policy, education, law, and legislation. Ever growing in the United States of America, the awareness of ACES as a public health crisis has also taken hold internationally.

The original study focused on the following adversities—emotional, physical, and sexual abuse; mother treated violently in the household; substance abuse in the household; mental illness in the household; parental separation and divorce; incarcerated parent in the household. More currently, the scenarios of adversity have been expanded to include a plethora of adverse experiences such as witnessing a sibling being abused, witnessing mutual combat between parents, community violence, being homeless, being the victim of sexual exploitation, involvement in the foster care system, losing a family member to deportation. Although suffering should not be compared, experiencing the insidious, daily effects of structural and systemic racism are now included as important adversities.

The "nature-nurture" debate has taken on new dimensions with the ACES study. Not only do adverse childhood experiences cause physical illness, but they also damage the hearts and souls of children. Early exposure to severe stress impacts brain development and its structure. A newer concept, toxic stress has emerged. This experience is characterized by a flood of hormones—adrenalin, cortisol—coursing through one's body and brain. Think of the flight, fright, and freeze responses associated with trauma. Particularly problematic is the fact that toxic stress has a pervasive life of its own and is unremitting. It is pernicious.

As devastating as adverse childhood experiences and toxic stress are, there is much evidence for the mitigation of its effects. Both the brain and the body have a desire to heal. Consider the work which has been done with stroke victims and those with traumatic brain injury. Evidence suggests that healthy lifestyle changes in nutrition, exercise, and sleep hygiene are fundamental to a healing process. Mental health interventions contribute to a renewed spirit.

The value of nurturing and supportive relationships is also critical to well being. Recognizing and cultivating the "Five Protective Factors" as part of family wellness contributes to family adaptability in the face of crisis. Parental adaptability, social connections; having concrete support in times of need; knowledge of positive parenting and child development, tending to the social and emotional competence of children—all are included in the collection of attributes which bolster family resilience. There are times when the family protective factors are compromised. There is no manual or college degree offered in positive parenting. Becoming a parent is an exercise in trying to chart the unknown. Parents who have suffered their own adverse childhood experiences may be jeopardized. Living in current adversity—economic strife being a common one—takes its toll.

Please consider however that the family is not the only institution in which children reside. The average child spends 35 hours per week in school, not an insignificant amount of time. How might educational settings offer its own complement of protective factors. No one is suggesting that the family unit is replaceable, but there is hope that schools can offer students a milieu of safe haven. What might such a context include?

Following are some historical and contemporary examples of how a school can offer a safe haven for academic excellence in an environment which addresses the needs of the whole child with outreach and engagement to families and caregivers. These schools have become trauma informed institutions that emphasize the elements of knowledge, competence, and sensitivity to all of its members. No one–administrators, teachers, support staff, custodial help—is exempt from enacting the philosophical premise of well being for self and others in all interactions. Cultural humility and sensitivity are hallmarks for interactions. A trauma informed school is replete with systemic change.

The first hint of schools as safe havens came with the establishment of sanctuary, compassionate, and mindful schools. Sandra Bloom, MD, a psychiatrist from Drexel University, Philadelphia, Pennsylvania, is credited with being the founder of non-violent environments (Bloom, 1997). She understood that little learning could not take place in an environment which was unsafe. Similarly, compassionate schools have been established where the emphasis is on focus, resilience, empathy, and connection. Mindful schools highlight teaching practices aimed at being in the moment in order to mitigate the "fight, flight, and freeze" reactions associated with trauma and toxic stress.

More recently schools have been focusing on social emotional learning (SEL) curriculum. This activity based approach benefits students in understanding and applying knowledge and skills designed toward emotional regulation. Although there are "boxed sets and kits" emphasizing these skills, schools need not necessarily spend money for implementing a trauma informed approach. Everyday life experiences, current events, socio political occurrences, relevant issues on the human condition, issues pertinent to child and adolescent development—these are just a few of the topics which make for meaningful fodder for social emotional learning and the art of compassion.

Trauma-informed schools are process, not program, oriented. A significant hallmark to trauma informed schools is the commitment to accessing academic curriculum through providing the safe environment. Achievement is hampered when psycho social and emotional needs are not met. It is important to know that these schools are not devoid of a discipline policy; however, such practices are not shame and punished based. Compassion with consequences becomes the focus for effective ways of confronting challenging behaviors. Emotional intelligence coupled with academic achievement is a stellar combination of attributes in developing a bright mind within a human being. Adopting a stance of leadership which offers an interest in exploring challenging behavior with an inquiry of "what happened?" rather than "why did you do that?" sets a different tone for keeping conflict to a minimum.

How might these new perspectives on healthy schools enact such changes? Essential for buy in would be the cooperative efforts of both administrators and teachers in concert with the greater school community, especially families. Where can one start on one's own as a classroom teacher when the grand systemic change feels elusive? Here follow 10 initial thoughts to creating a safe haven within the classroom domain.

1. Establish the classroom community as a context of safe learning by keeping
the rules clear and understandable. Be confident, firm, and caring.

2. Allow for a range of verbal expression which is in keeping with the diverse
student cultures.

3. Adapt a stance whereby there is acceptance of the reality that the curriculum won't   become compromised for the time spent on classroom climate.

4. Offer flexibility in the lesson plan when learning is hampered by big feelings. Stop the flow and move to a conversation of restoration before returning to the lesson.

5. Provide a classroom space with small, anxiety reduction toys, often referred to as "fidgets." These small handheld items provide an outlet for excess energy. They
provide a filtering mechanism to channel the flow of extra sensory information without distracting the class at large.

6. Model and maintain a calm demeanor.

7. Establish a brief routine of community circles on a regular basis to allow for the expression of student concerns and provocative topics. A circle is formed with students facing inward, the safe enclosure, with guidelines for sharing and the allowance not to speak.

8. Strategically time brain breaks, brief periods away from the lesson, in order to offer students alternatives to sitting in one place. Stretching,

jogging in place, shaking one's hands, doing a dance move to music—all allow for blood to flow throughout the body and into the brain.

9. Consider opening and closing rituals at the beginning and ending of classes or activities to provide refocusing with transitions. Such practices might include a moment of quiet reflection, an opportunity to write on one's own current emotional state, listening to soothing music, listening to someone reading a poem. The list of these transitioning exercises is endless.

10. Implement social emotional learning activities on a routine basis.

The suggestions above allow for teacher and student adaptability throughout the day.

If the belief is that there are no students who have experienced adversity and that toxic stress does not impact the lives of students, then what would be the harm in adopting a philosophy whereby the emotional health of students and staff is valued with the same regard as academic excellence? There is a strong possibility that, if trauma informed schools were the norm, this specialized environment would counter the need to introduce or shift the focus of the school in times of disaster.

PART 3: COPING STRATEGIES FOR THE SCHOOL-FAMILY COMMUNITY

HOW PRINCIPALS CAN PROMOTE COMMUNICATION AND CONNECTION DURING A DISASTER

Our schools are the center of a community. All members of the community, students, teachers, staff and families share a commitment of working together toward a common goal of educating all students in a caring, trusting environment. As the school leader, Principals have an awesome responsibility during "normal" times, and even more so during times such as this unprecedented pandemic crisis, other tragedies or natural disasters. The role of the school principal in the midst of these challenges is multi-faceted and can be at times daunting. As leaders, Principals during these crises, will need to muster their intellect, their many skills, and build on the strength of their relationships within the school community to address the complicated problems that arrive often without warning. On the one hand, the Principal must immediately manage logistics, the day to day operations of the school, particularly those requiring the numerous steps to operationalize new modes of conducting daily instruction and activities.

At the same time, the Principal must address the many needs of the staff and community and find ways to make needed changes to improve all aspects of the school during this crisis, oftentimes establishing new traditions or the new normal. This includes professional development for teachers, access to technology, supplies, and possibly meals for students. The immediate needs of staff, students and families requires developing channels of communication to inform and support. It is the Principal's responsibility to provide members of the school community with the information and resources they need to maintain an atmosphere conducive to teaching and learning.

However, in addition to managing the wide range of actions needed to keep a school functioning during extraordinary times, Principals are also called upon to provide emotional support and connection to the various members of the community. How can Principals be proactive in providing that support and reassurance to students, staff and families, acknowledging their needs and searching for ways to address them? The following suggestions may assist you in developing action steps for supporting your school community during a disaster:

COMMUNICATION

Communication is the driver in providing support and reassurance to the school community. Providing data and facts, sharing plans and giving encouragement has special meaning when a crisis strikes. Establishing regular and ongoing communication among and between all members of the school community is the glue that keeps all informed, engaged and connected.

Deliver regular, ongoing communication by providing:

Accessibility to the Principal and Staff: Letting the school community know you and your staff are available. Establish systems for direct communication with a commitment to quick response as much as possible. Help students, teachers and families feel comfortable and at ease. Be kind, calm and compassionate.

Information: Being a conduit for information from the school district as well as specific updates regarding your school. Informative email blasts and robo-calls to staff and families keep everyone updated on important information and circumstances, particularly in the early stages of a crisis. Parents will feel reassured that the school is doing all it can to be informative, to connect, to establish and/or maintain routine and structure, with regard for student wellbeing and safety being of utmost importance.

Weekly Bulletins for Students and Families: Establish or continue regular weekly bulletins. Usually bulletins include activities, event information and notices and gives students opportunities to participate in extra-curricular activities. Supporting the new normal of the school community requires creative ways to maintain student involvement and engagement.

Examples of Virtual Events: Virtual Variety Show; Poster, Poetry or Essay Contest to Celebrate a Special Holiday; Cultural Events such as Lunar New Year, Cinco de Mayo, Black History Month, Spring. Keeping in touch with faculty and staff during online, regular faculty meetings and professional development activities. Include a check-in process, inviting faculty members to share thoughts and feelings, concerns or make suggestions and requests. Demonstrate empathy by being responsive to their needs, and follow up with teachers on an individual basis when you determine there is a need for additional support.

Faculty communiques: A faculty bulletin can become a way to encourage and inspire staff during a crises: to keep going, support their students and colleagues, build resilience and healthy self-care practices. Possible guidelines for supporting their students include talking to students about the crisis, about what is happening and share possible coping strategies. Avoiding talking about the crisis may give students a message of being unwilling to be of assistance. Also, alert faculty to watch for changes in behavior among their students- from stress-related symptoms to difficulty concentrating or physical symptoms. Work in tandem with school mental health professionals to provide the assistance students may need.

CONNECTION AND ENGAGEMENT

In a prolonged time of crisis, it can be challenging for schools to remain connected to members of the community. How can students be reassured, motivated to succeed under difficult circumstances? How can teachers meet student needs while learning remotely? These are things that Principals can address by facilitating connection and engagement in the school community.

Reach out to students

Continuity of student support activities: School support staff may need guidance to provide students with ongoing emotional support activities, though virtual. For example, many schools have supportive "Lunch Bunch" or Support Groups, as well as a Wellness Program to assist students with managing stress, anxiety, grief, etc., or health needs on an individual basis. Staff may need support finding ways to continue to provide these important services during a crisis. Collaborating with the Principal to establish ways to inform staff and students of services available is required in order to continue to meet student needs.

Principal chats: On a regular basis, provide groups of students with an opportunity to meet with the principal, if necessary, virtually. Give them an opportunity to talk about their thoughts and feelings. Ask them what they already know and listen to their individual concerns. Provide realistic, but not false, reassurance to help them feel a connection to their school and fellow students.

Student Surveys: Reach out to students to take a pulse of how students are managing and feeling at various times during the year. Share results and analyze data with staff to inform data-driven next steps with staff.

Materials and Supply distribution: While there is a task at hand, namely to get materials to students, this can also be expanded to be an opportunity to check-in with students face to face. As teachers connect with their students, encourage them to provide students with honest, realistic reassurances about the hope for the future of school life.

Reach out to families
Town Hall Meetings: An opportunity for community input. With diverse needs and communities, arrange multiple meetings either by grade levels, language groups or interest levels. Sensitivity to scheduling times is important to maximum participation.

Home Visits: Support teams, lead by the Principal, can reach out to identify and support students who are not attending school due to a lack of resources, academic support, home problems or illness. The team can assist the student's needs and will provide the necessary materials or services to assure the student resumes regular school attendance.

Virtual Parent-Teacher Organization Meetings: With the help of more formal parent-teacher organizations, this group can provide opportunities for parents to help the school community and give support to teachers. Being able to assist others during a crisis helps us feel less powerless and perhaps feel a little better.

SELF-CARE
'We are all in this together.' Take the lead when necessary, however, share leadership roles and responsibilities with members of the community when feasible. Asking for help is not a sign of weakness.

- Find support and consultation with trusted colleague Principals through regular check-ins. Brainstorm solutions to issues and questions by discussions with your thought partners.

- You can't do it all at once. Prioritize your tasks, maintain school routine and structure to maintain a sense of calm.
- Be compassionate and kind to yourself and others. Together you will find your way through this difficult time.

Principals who are sensitive to the pressures and anxieties experienced by the school community during a crisis will make decisions based on actively listening to community needs. They will then take steps to meet those needs while keeping in mind the limits of their resources and personal skills and talents . Networking with the broader school system and the community-at-large can support Principal's actions while sharing the burden of meeting the school's needs with positive and caring results.

HOW TEACHERS CAN SUPPORT FAMILIES DURING A DISASTER

Disasters affect families as well as individual children. Parents serve as a buffer for child stress and have a critical role in disaster response and management (Tambling et al., 2020). Family efficacy and resilience are affected by various factors like family demographics, parents' reactions, the quality of parent-child relationships and interactions and parenting style. Naturally, these factors influence children's reaction to disaster and recovery. We recognize that many teachers may object to having a more active role with parents as "not being a legitimate part of the role of a teacher." However, there is extensive research demonstrating that parent involvement with schools is a critical factor in promoting children's academic success and that a positive teacher-parent relationship facilitates that academic success.

This section will emphasize strategies teachers can use to strengthen: (1) parents' self-efficacy (2) parent-child interaction, and (3) family functioning as a unit.

Here are some tips for teacher-parent communication during a disaster, based on the following assumptions (Wisner, 2018):

- The teacher's challenge is to communicate with parents in a way that does not merely transmit information or give instruction, but also facilitates communication among family members.

- In order to achieve a sense of resilience, collaboration between teacher and parents is required. It is the teacher's responsibility to try to recruit and work with children and their families.

- Communication with children and their families should not be one-way since parents and children possess their own perceptions and ideas and therefore, should be interlocutors.

- Children play an important role in bringing disaster risk awareness home with them from school, encouraging their families to make plans and take preparedness.

How can teachers strengthen parents' self-efficacy?

Children look up to their parents searching for cues of how to act, especially in time of disaster and high stressful time. How parents' function during and after the disaster has significant influence on how children respond. Therefore, parents must first cope with their own stress and tend to their own emotional experience and self-care related to the crisis. For example, in a stressful situation during a flight, the parents should be the first one to put on the oxygen mask before taking care of their children. It is the teachers' role to support parents in this process. As explained in the next paragraph.

a) Teacher-parents informal talk initiated on a regular basis by the teacher, may help the teacher to find out how the parents feel and how family elements in the children's immediate context support or not support effective coping.

Examples for informal teacher-parent conversation questions:
Hi Carol (always contact the parent by his first name) how are you? How are you doing these days? How do you cope with the current challenges? Is anyone helping you? Is there anything you would like to ask or consult with me about? How do you think your child copes with the situation? How do you and your child get along under the circumstances? Is there anything you would have liked to change? Is there anything I can do to help?
It is not only the contents of the conversation but especially the teacher's willingness to listen to the parent, which is of great importance.

b) To empower the parents and to instill a sense of hope and avoid a sense of despair it is important to help parents to be proactive and not passive.

Teachers can share assignments with parents.
For example, if the parent shares with the teacher his difficulty with his child (e.g., wetting at night, reluctance to attend an online class, the child's difficulty getting up in the morning, or the child's anxieties), teachers and parents can work together to identify possible solutions such as referral to a school mental health professional and set regular times for follow-up.

c) Sharing emotions: the teacher can recommend parents to establish parents' group support by WhatsApp or any other social network and application for correspondence. It can be used for sharing emotions, hopes and reliable information.

How can a teacher strengthen parent-child interaction?
Children might be particularly vulnerable to serious mental health consequences associated with the crisis. Parents are the significant figures in the child's immediate environment, and they have an important role in scaffolding and being role model for child's stress management. Therefore, it is so important to help parents to strengthen their rapport with their children.

A contact notebook: parents and children can keep a notebook in which they exchange messages. For example, each one in his turn will write three good things that happened during the passing day.

Notes with short positive statements: the teacher can recommend to parents to write inspiring and positive notes that will be attached to the refrigerator or put under the pillow or next to the toothpaste (e.g., *I love you; Yes, we can!; You look wonderful with the mask; thank you for helping prepare dinner etc.,*). Parents can also write down family jokes or riddles. It should be noted that parents and children should exchange mutual notes.

How can a teacher encourage a family to function as a unit?
Researchers point out four factors in the children's immediate family context of parents, siblings, extended family, and pets that appear essential to their capacity to cope with a crisis: a sense of protection, reassurance, re-establishment of routines and stability (Mooney, 2017).

Establishment of routines: one of the most popular family routines in Israel is meeting for a family meal at least once a week. The teacher can recommend that parents add a meaning to the family meetings (e.g., each family member will share an amusing incident or a good thing that happened to him/her during the week; each family member will thank someone or something that happened during the passing week; or dedicate an object, real or imaginary to another member in the family).

To sum up, teachers have the knowledge and resources to support parents during disasters and consequently parents will serve as role models, providing backing and support for their children.

CONCLUSION

We were encouraged to write this manual because of two things. First, our own experiences as educators which have taught us that it is a privilege to teach and be involved in schools, and that schools are community centers of learning and hope. Second, we regard the evidence-based support represented in the studies shown in Appendix 1 as a powerful testament to the healing power of schools during a disaster. We hope that this manual has been helpful to you and your school. At our website disastershock.com you will find additional resources that may be of assistance to your school community.

REFERENCES

Berger, E., Carroll, M., Maybery, D. & Harrison, D. (2018). Disaster Impacts on Students and Staff from a Specialist, Trauma-Informed Australian School. *Journal of Child & Adolescent Trauma*, *11*, 521–530. doi: 10.1007/s40653-018-0228-6

Bloom, S. L. (1997). *Creating sanctuary: Toward the evolution of sane societies*. Psychology Press.

Brymer M., Taylor, M., Escudero, P., Jacobs, A., Kronenberg, M., Macy, R., Mock, L., Payne, L., Pynoos, R., & Vogel, J. (2012). *Psychological First Aid for schools: Field operations guide, 2nd Edition*. Los Angeles: National Child Traumatic Stress Network.

Cohen, J., Goodman, R., Kliethermes, M. D., & Epstein, C. (2020). *Helping Children with Traumatic Separation or Traumatic Grief Related to COVID-19*. Los Angeles, CA, and Durham, NC: National Center for Child Traumatic Stress.

Cotman, C. W., Berchtold, N. C. & Christie, L. A. (2007). Exercise builds brain health: key roles of Growth factor cascades and inflammation. *Trends Neurosci*; *30*(9):464-72. doi: 10.1016/j.tins.2007.06.011

Gerrard, B., Girault, E., Appleton, V. Giraudo, S., and Linville Shaffer, S. (2020). *Disastershock: How to cope with the emotional stress of a major disaster*. Stuart, FL: Institute for School-Based Family Counseling. Retrieved from https://www.disastershock.com/download

Halladay Goldman, J., Danna, L., Maze, J. W., Pickens, I. B., & Ake III, G. S. (2020). *Trauma Informed School Strategies during COVID-19.* Los Angeles, CA, and Durham, NC: National Center for Child Traumatic Stress.

Hunter, M. R., Gillespie, B. W. & Chen, S.Y. (2019). Urban Nature Experiences Reduce Stress in the Context of Daily Life Based on Salivary Biomarkers. *Frontiers in Psychol*ogy, *10*:722. doi: 10.3389/fpsyg.2019.00722

Jaycox, L. H., Morse, L. K., Tanielian, T. & Stein, B. D. (2006). *How Schools Can Help Students Recover from Traumatic Experiences*. Santa Monica, CA: RAND Corporation.

Mooney, M., Tarrant, R., Paton, D., Johal, S., & Johnston, D. (2017). Getting through: Children's effective coping and adaptation in the context of the Canterbury, New Zealand, Earthquakes of 2010-2012. *Australasian Journal of Disaster and Trauma Studies*, 21(1), 19-30.

National Child Traumatic Stress Network, Schools Committee. (2017). *Creating, supporting, and sustaining trauma-informed schools: A system framework.* Los Angeles, CA, and Durham, NC: National Center for Child Traumatic Stress.

Pfefferbaum, B., Pfefferbaum, R. L. & Van Horn, R. L. (2018). Involving children in disaster risk reduction: the importance of participation. *European Journal of Psychotraumatology, 9:2*, 1425577. doi:10.1080/20008198.2018.1425577

Pfefferbaum, B., Sweeton, J. L., Newman, E., Varma, V., Nitiéma, P., Shaw, J. A., Chrisman, A. K. & Noffsinger, M. A. (2014). Child disaster mental health interventions, part I, *Disaster Health, 2:1*, 46-57. doi: 10.4161/dish.27534

Pfefferbaum, B., Sweeton, J. L., Newman, E., Varma, V., Nitiéma, P., Shaw, J. A.,

Chrisman, A. K. & Noffsinger, M. A. (2014). Child disaster mental health interventions, part II, *Disaster Health, 2:1*, 58-67. doi: 10.4161/dish.27535

Rechtschaffen, D. (2014). *The Way of Mindful Education: Cultivating Well-Being in Teachers and Students.* US, New York: WW Norton & Co.

Tambling, R. R., Tomkunas, A. J., Russell, B. S., Horton, A. L., & Hutchison, M. (2020). Thematic analysis of parent–child conversations about COVID-19: "Playing It Safe". *Journal of Child and Family Studies*,30, 1-13.
Tobin, J. (2019, June 19). *Educational continuity: The role of schools in facilitating disaster recovery.* Natural Hazards Center. Retrieved from https://hazards.colorado.edu/news/research-counts/educational-continuity-the-role-of- schools-in-facilitating-disaster-recovery

Yanev, P., & Thompson, A. C. (2009). *Peace of mind in earthquake country: How to save your home, business, and life.* Chronicle Books.

Wisner, B., Paton, D., Alisic, E., Eastwood, O., Shreve, C., & Fordham, M. (2018). Communication with children and families about disaster: reviewing multi-disciplinary literature 2015–2017. *Current psychiatry reports*, 20(9), 1-9.

Appendix 1: Studies on the Calming Role School Personnel Have on Children Coping with Disasters and Trauma

Alisic, E., Bus, M., Dulack, W., Pennings, L. & Splinter, J. (2012). Teachers' experiences supporting children after traumatic exposure. *Journal of Traumatic Stress*. 25 (1), 98-101.

Berger, R., Gelkopf, M. (2009). School-based intervention for the treatment of tsunami-related distress in children: A quasi-randomized controlled trial. *Psychotherapy and Psychosomatics*. 78, 364–371.

Jaycox, L.H., Morse, L.K., Tanielian, T., & Stein, B.D. (2006). How Schools Can Help Students Recover from Traumatic Experiences: A Tool Kit for Supporting Long-Term Recovery. Santa Monica, CA: RAND Corporation. Retrieved from http://www.rand.org/content/dam/rand/pubs/technical_reports/2006/RAND_TR413.pdf.

Johnson, V. & Ronan, K. (2014). Classroom responses of New Zealand school teachers following the 2011 Christchurch earthquake. *Natural Hazards* 72(2):1075-1092

Le Brocque, R., De Young, A., Montague, G., Pocock, S., March, S., Triggell, N., Rabaa, C. & Kenardy, J. (2017). Schools and natural disaster recovery: The unique and vital role that teachers and education professionals play in ensuring the mental health of students following natural disasters. *Journal of Psychologists and Counsellors in Schools*, 27 (1), 1-23.

Minahan, Jesica (2019). Trauma-Informed Teaching Strategies. *Educational Leadership*. 77 (2), 30-35.

Ophir, Y., Rosenberg, H., Asterhan, C. & Schwarz, B. (2016). In times of war, adolescents do not fall silent: Teacher - student social network communication in wartime. *Journal of Adolescence*. 46, 98-106.

Plumb, J., Bush, K. & Kersevich, S. (2016). Trauma-sensitive schools: An evidence-based approach. *School Social Work Journal*. 40 (2), 37-60.

Stevens, J.E. (2012, Jun 26). Trauma-sensitive schools are better schools. *Huffington Post*. Retrieved from http://www.huffingtonpost.com/jane-ellen-stevens/trauma-sensitive-schools_b_1625924.html.

Teaching Tolerance Staff (2020). A trauma-informed approach to teaching through coronavirus. Retrieved from https://www.tolerance.org/magazine/a-trauma-informed-approach-to-teaching-through-coronavirus

Wisconsin Department of Public Instruction (2013). Mental Health: Creating Trauma-Sensitive Schools to Improve Learning: A Response to Intervention (RtI) Model. Retrieved from http://sspw.dpi.wi.gov/sspw_mhtrauma.

Wolmer, L., Hamiel, D. & Laor, N. (2011). Preventing children's posttraumatic stress after disaster with teacher-based intervention: A controlled study. *Journal of the American Academy of Child & Adolescent Psychiatry*. 50 (4), 340-348.

Zhu, Z., Wang, R., Kao, H., Zong, Y., Liu, Z., Tang, S., Xu, M., Liu, I. & Lam, S. (2014). Effect of calligraphy training on hyperarousal symptoms for childhood survivors of the 2008 China earthquakes. *Neuropsychiatric Disease and Treatment*. 10, 977-985.

Disastershock Educator Collaboration Team Authors

Introduction: The Critical Role of Schools in Coping with Disaster
Karen Buchanan, EdD School of Education, George Fox University, Oregon, USA
Thomas Buchanan, EdD School of Education, George Fox University, Oregon, USA

Part 1 Coping Strategies for School Personnel
How to Identify When School Personnel are Stressed
Suzanne Giraudo, PhD Clinical Director of the California Pacific Medical Center
Department of Pediatrics Child Development Center, San Francisco, California, USA

Why is Teacher Self-Care Important?*
Justin Kenardy, PhD, Emeritus professor, School of Psychology, Faculty of Health and
Behavioural Sciences, University of Queensland, Brisbane, Australia
Alexandra De Young, PhD., School of Psychology, Faculty of Health and Behavioural
Sciences, University of Queensland, Brisbane, Australia
Robyne Le Brocque, PhD, School of Nursing, Midwifery and Social Work, Faculty of Health
and Sciences, University of Queensland, Brisbane, Australia
Rod Marsh, PhD, Queensland Brain Institute, University of Queensland, Brisbane,
Australia

10 Methods for School Personnel to Cope with Disaster Stress
Brian Gerrard, PhD Chief Academic Officer, Western Institute for Social Research,
Berkeley, California, USA,

Part 2 Coping Strategies for Students
How to Identify When Students are Stressed
Suzanne Giraudo, PhD Clinical Director of the California Pacific Medical Center
Department of Pediatrics Child Development Center, San Francisco, California, USA

Teaching Strategies for Reducing Student Stress
Celina Korzeniowski, PhD, National Scientific and Technical Research Council of Argentina
(CONICET- Argentina) and Faculty of Psychology, Aconcagua University, Mendoza,
Argentina

Classroom Expectations and Management During a Disaster*
Justin Kenardy, PhD, Emeritus professor, School of Psychology, Faculty of Health and
Behavioural Sciences, University of Queensland, Brisbane, Australia
Alexandra De Young, PhD., School of Psychology, Faculty of Health and Behavioural
Sciences, University of Queensland, Brisbane, Australia
Robyne Le Brocque, PhD, School of Nursing, Midwifery and Social Work, Faculty of Health
and Behavioural Sciences, University of Queensland, Brisbane, Australia

Rod Marsh, PhD, Queensland Brain Institute, University of Queensland, Brisbane, Australia

How Teachers Can Use the Expressive Arts to Help Students Cope
Bridget Steed, MA, LMHC Mental Health Counselor, Oregon, USA

Schoolchildren as Resources for Overcoming a Disaster Crisis
Masamine Jimba, MD, Department of Community and Global Health, Graduate School of Medicine, The University of Tokyo, Tokyo, Japan

How a Trauma Informed School Benefits Students
Toni Nemia, MA, LMFT Executive Director, Center for Child & Family Development, Western Institute for Social Research, Berkeley, California;Retired teacher with the San Francisco Unified School District, San Francisco, California, USA

Part 3 Coping Strategies for the School-Family Community
How Principals Can Promote Communication and Connection During a Disaster
Judy Giampaoli, LMFT, Lately: Principal: Francisco Middle School, San Francisco; Member: Advisory Board Center for Child & Family Development, Western Institute for Social Research, Berkeley, California, USA

How Teachers Can Support Families During Disaster
Nurit Kaplan Toren, PhD, Oranim Academic College of Education, Faculty of Graduate Studies and Education and University of Haifa, Israel
Jaffa Weiss, M.Ed, Former high school principal, Israel

* Reprinted and adapted with permission from
Childhood Trauma Reactions: A guide for Educators from Preschool to Year 12, by Kenardy, J.A., De Young, A., Le Brocque, R., & March, S. 2011, Brisbane, Australia. Centre of National Research on Disability and Rehabilitation Medicine, University of Queensland.

****

If you would like to give us feedback on our book, we would really appreciate it.

Please send your comments and suggestions to:
Dr. Brian Gerrard gerrardba@outlook.com

Additional Reading for Parents and Adults working with Children:
Available on KOBO, Amazon, and free download with
translations in 26 languages at disastershock.com

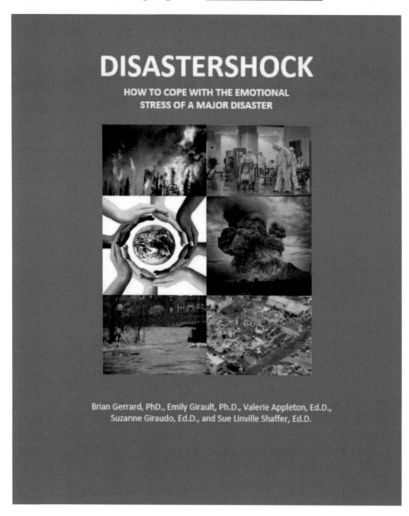

Made in the USA
Las Vegas, NV
25 April 2021